my name is big

Lazarus Lake

Illustrations by Betsy Julian

laz.btsgifts.com
drystoneman@hotmail.com

First Printed Edition, March 2012

Printed in the United States of America
Print ISBN-10: 1470091178
Print ISBN-13: 978-1470091170

Illustrations by Betsy Julian
Cover Design by Blaine Moore
Published by Trail Trotter Press / Run to Win, LLC (the "Publisher").

Trail Trotter Press
824 Roosevelt Trail #203
Windham, ME, 04062
www.TrailTrotterPress.com

Table of Contents

Prologue:

This is Big Dog's story. It is the story of a big ugly dog in a hostile world. It is the story of a dog who was abused, abandoned, shot, and left for dead, yet persevered to make himself a home. It is the story of the triumph of a gentle, intelligent, loving giant who never gave up.

As a lifelong marathon and ultramarathon runner, I belong to a community which keeps in touch and exchanges information on the internet, by way of the Ultralist. Most of the posts on the ultralist deal strictly with ultramarathons, but some whim compelled me to post about my first meeting with the dog that would come to be known as simply "the Big."

After I took him to the vet, instead of turning him over to animal control, I thought I had made a mistake. I was not sure where I would get the money to cover his medical bills. It was like a miracle when donations to help with Big's expenses began to come from other members of the list, most of them people I had never met.

In return, I felt obligated to post a few updates about Big's progress. One thing led to another, and I had no choice but to keep the listers apprised about the continuing adventures of their Big Dog.

Over the next year and a half, the Big Dog's life went through many twists and turns. He found a new "permanent" home in St. Louis. He was abandoned again in Nashville, where he spent a couple of miserable months chained in a yard. Ultimately he ended up back at our house on the hill, way out in the woods.

Through it all, Big's growing community of friends and supporters on the Ultralist followed the posts about his many adventures. Before it was all over, there was a Big Dog Trailrunners club, sporting their Big Dog T-shirts around the country, and even the world.

A trail was built around our farm, and named the Big Trail, on which was held an ultramarathon race; the Big Dog Backyard Ultra. The dog who once had no one had developed a community of friends thanks to the continuing posts to the Ultralist.

Those posts are what make up this book. This is not a work of fine literature. These are Big Dog's stories.

part 1: rescue

my name is big

hello. my name is big.
master says i owe my life to you.
so i want to thank you.
i do not know you,
but master says when i was hurt you paid for my vet bills,
and my medicine to make me better.
i do not know why strangers would do these things for me.
but i am grateful.

that was a scary time.
i used to have a different master and a different name.

one day that master took me in the car.
we drove far away to a place i had never been.
master & i got out,
then master forgot and drove away without me.

i had never been alone outside before.
and i was very afraid.
so i waited for master to come back for me.
i waited all day.
i got very hungry and thirsty.
but i dared not leave. master left me there
so that must be where i was supposed to stay.
finally a car came.
it wasn't master, but it was a human.
i needed help and humans are help.
i do not know why, but he was afraid.
he yelled at me and threw rocks.
so i ran away.
i found another human
and i went to him for help.
this one pointed a stick at me and fire came out of it.
my shoulder exploded with pain and my leg wouldn't work.
so i ran on 3 legs, back to where the master left me.
the rock throwing human was gone, but his car was there.
so i hid in the woods nearby, under a fallen tree.
and i waited for master to come back.

all night i lay there.
and all the next day.
my leg was on fire.
i was so hungry, and so thirsty,
but master never came.
another night went by, and another day.
each morning the rock throwing human left
each afternoon he came back.
i was weak and feverish.
all my world was hunger, thirst, and pain.
i needed my master.

then the rock thrower came back again.
this time he saw me.
he came towards me, and i was afraid.
i wanted to run, but i was so weak.
so i just wagged my tail to beg him not to hurt me.
if he will leave me here, master will come to save me.

he did not hurt me.
he talked to me in a kind voice, then he left.
in a few minutes he came back with some food.
he put the food nearby and stepped away.
so i got up and came out to eat.
after i started to eat, he walked away.

i had a difficult choice.
i was hungry, and there was food.
but i needed help and humans are help.
this kind human was leaving.
so i left the food and followed him the best i could,
with my injured leg and the sickness and weakness.
he let me follow until we came to the house.
then he closed the door on me.

i needed to go inside. i was an inside dog.
i was afraid to be outside alone.

in a few minutes he came back with more food,
and some water.

so i finally got to eat and drink.
afterwards i lay down and watched the door.

every so often i saw the kind human look out at me.
each time i was ready to wag my tail for him.
finally i fell asleep.

the next day the kind human gave me more water
then he led me to a car.
he tried to get me to go inside,
but i remembered what happened with master.
i did not want to get inside.
that did not matter, as the kind human spoke to me
then picked me up and put me inside.

once again we drove a long way
to an unfamiliar place.
the kind human petted me and spoke in a soothing tone
but i was afraid.

he took me out in a place with many dogs (and nasty cats).
a kind lady took my leash and led me away.
so many strangers and strange animals were all around.
the lady put a needle in me, and i went to sleep.

when i awoke, i was in a small cage
surrounded by other cages with other dogs.
i was lonesome and afraid.
my leg hurt very bad.
but i got water and food and no one was mean to me.

later i was sitting in my cage
when i heard a familiar voice outside.
it was the kind human.
i barked as loud as i could, so he would find me.
it worked, and soon he put me in the car
and took me back to his house.

since then my life has been very happy.
my new master takes good care of me.

every morning, when the sun comes up,
he comes and gets me on my pretty blue leash.

i have a lot of important work to do.
i must sit still and not jump while he gets me.
i have to walk right beside him
and go up the steps one at a time,
after master goes up first.
i must sit and be good until master tells me it is ok to eat.
then we take a long walk if i do good.
(or a short walk if i forget how to act)
no matter how i do, at the end master pets me and praises me.
my life is very happy.

all day long, the dog named little comes out and stays with me.
sometimes we play.
sometimes we nap.
but we have a good time all day.

in the evening master returns.
first little has to do her work.
then i do mine.
it is satisfying to have important work to do.
at the end, he pets me and holds me,
and tells me what a good dog i am.

one day i realized that my name is big.
when master says big dog, or big boy, or big fella,
he means me.
when i hear him say big it makes me happy all over
and i can feel my tail wagging from the pleasure.

all these good things have happened
because humans i do not know cared about me.

my name is big.
and i want to thank you for my good life.

big dog

may 18, 2010
act of faith

last friday, when i came driving up to the house after work,
a big, ugly dog came running around from the front yard.

and i mean a BIIIIG UUUUGLY dog.
about an 80 pound, red pit bull.
it stopped a little ways from my car door,
and looked at me.

most dogs have those big brown heart-melting eyes.
this dog had those green-yellow eyes,
that look like they belong to some sort of a demon.

looking at it, i could see the indention around its neck
where a too tight collar had once been
"great" i thought to myself.
"some idiot feels the need to own a killer,
and now it is loose in my yard."

still, it hadn't gotten all the way to the car.
actually, its behavior had all been submissive,
wagging its tail, and dipping its head.
so i cracked the door a little and shouted out,
"GET OUT OF HERE!"

the dog backed up a couple of steps.

so i got out and yelled more bravely,
"GO ON HOME, GET OUT OF HERE!"
the dog started down the driveway,
glancing over its shoulder at me.
i picked up a rock and chucked it at the dog.

i missed, but the dog sped up to a full run.
part of me was admiring the beauty and power of the animal
but the rest of me was chucking another rock,
hoping to make connection and discourage it from ever coming
back.

that attended to, i went to see if little dog was all right.
i was afraid that bloodthirsty monster might have killed her.

little was fine, and when i took her out for her walk
we saw the big red dog down by the road.

it looked at me hopefully,
but i just warned it off.
i was brave, once i found out it was afraid of me.

i stopped and talked to a couple of kids riding bikes, to see if they
knew whose dog it was.
they only knew of one pit bull, belonging to someone named
bubba. but that dog was "really mean. it is a bad, bad dog."
no, the dog in my yard had not been a mean dog.

one of them, maybe 8 years old, volunteered proudly,
"my uncle had a pit bull. it was a great dog. it won 26 fights in a
row. then it lost. when he got home, he threw it in the ditch and
shot it in the head!"

my stomach clenched. not for the dog, but for the kid.
he doesn't even know this is wrong.
what chance does he really have in life?
about the same as that dog.

i saw another neighbor driving by in a truck
(one that i knew had a smaller pit bull that he kept in his yard).
i flagged him down, but he also had no idea where the big dog
had come from.

i didn't see it when i got home. i didn't see it saturday, when me
& little dog were doing our chores.
(alright, maybe i do most of the chores, and the dog is little help.
but i like having her along)

but sunday, when i got home from work, i saw something move
in the edge of the woods, under a fallen tree trunk that was
suspended between other trees.
when i looked more intently, i could see it was the big red dog.

10

i went to get a closer look, and the dog struggled to its feet...
3 of them.
someone had shot it in the chest,
and one foreleg stuck out at an angle, useless.

well, crap.

i guess i will have to call animal control tomorrow.
meantime, i went and got a bowl of little dog's food.
no need for the animal to suffer any more than i can help.

when i took out the food, i tried not to look.
but there was no missing the pleading look
(even in those devil eyes).
he began eating greedily, but when i started for the house,
he came limping along behind.

well, crap again.

it is supposed to come a gully washer tonight. i reckon he would
be miserable laying out there in the rain, hurt.
"come on big dog. you might as well spend your last night on the
porch, where it is dry."

once up on the porch, little dog was going nuts,
running in circles and banging into the big dog.
i warned her,
"little, that dog could bite you in two with one chomp!"
little didn't care, and the big dog gave no sign of aggression.
actually, he looked like he would like to play if he weren't
injured.

so i let him sniff my hand, and then petted his head.
his joy was palpable.
as purely ugly as the dog is, it is a good natured animal.
whoever had this dog, it must not have been mistreated.
well, until they dumped it on my farm.
but it is easy to imagine a thousand scenarios where a giant pit
bull would not be welcome, and a good natured dog like this
would be hard to put down.
(yeah, you have to be heartless, like me, to pull that off)

as the night went on, about every 30 minutes i would go over and look out the door. the big dog lying on the welcome mat would bob its head with joy and wag its tail. there was a swelling around the bullet hole the size of a softball.

finally, i gave up and called the vet.
"i just want to see if she can do something to ease its suffering tonight," i lied to myself. "i can still call animal control to come get it in the morning."

the vet was unable to do anything that night, as she was out of town at a horse show. but i found myself making arrangements to bring the big dog by her office first thing the next morning. i went to the porch and patted the dog, promising him, "you live until morning, and we will see if we can't do something to help you out."

it wasn't until this morning that i thought,
"now how the heck am i gonna get this creature to the vet?"
it would be quite a trick to lift the animal if he wasn't hurt, and picking up an injured animal capable of crushing my entire head in its jaws is not on my list of smart things to do. so there was no way to put it in the back of my truck. the only option left was to load him in the front seat of my car with me.

apparently his last car ride had not ended well.
the big dog balked at getting in the car.
i coaxed and pleaded.
i tempted him with food.
he would look in the door, but he wasn't about to get in.

finally, i told him, "well, big dog. i am going to have to pick you up and put you in the car. i hope you know this is an act of faith that you wont kill me."
then i picked up his rear end, and pushed him in.

when i got in the car with him, i realized just how freaking big he really is. he barely fit in the passenger side of the car, and his head, the size of a bowling ball, was about 18 inches from mine. "i sure hope you don't flip out when i start the car," i told him, "because if you do, i am a dead man."

it wasn't until the vets office that the truth dawned on me
after telling her i was only looking for an evaluation.
the severity of the injury, the age of the dog, and the potential
cost of treatment, naturally, i had to fill out paperwork, accepting
financial responsibility.
when i got to the line asking for "pet name",
i hesitated, then i wrote in "Big Dog"

oh heck. now he has a name.
i went on to work,
but all day long i kept wondering what would be the word.

the word is: he is less than a year old
(my god, that goliath is a puppy!)
and they wont know till tomorrow whether they can save his leg
or not.

only two months ago i had my own leg surgery,
ending more than 40 years as a runner.
how could i turn my back on a leg-issues brother?
i think the big dog has found a home.

i promise you that i am not some old softy. there have been a
number of dumped puppies since little dog, and i haven't even
considered keeping a one of them. but it isn't the cute puppies
that get to me. it is the dogs i know no one else would ever want.
i guess i can identify with them.

laz

may 19, 2010
more updates than you can shake a stick at

based on the inquiries, i think the first update that people are interested in has to be the big dog.

big dog is a very lucky dog.
the bullet (meant to kill him) clipped the humerus.
apparently, it was some sort of hollow point, meant to explode when it hit something solid, and do maximum damage.
the humerus, being the thickest bone in the shoulder, sustained damage in the form of a big chunk knocked out, but the many fragments of bullet did all their damage in the massive musculature of big dog's shoulder. by a pure miracle, the bone structure is largely undamaged.

had it been a solid projectile, it would have penetrated on into the chest cavity, and probably had a fatal result.
big dog is a very lucky dog.

2 days of confinement have allowed the shoulder to start a healing process. the feared nerve damage, because of the way the leg was sticking out and not moving, appears to be at the worst not complete damage. big dog is moving that leg again, altho still not bearing any weight on it.

the current plan of treatment is heavy antibiotics, and continued confinement to allow the shoulder to heal. if big dog's luck holds out, the body will isolate all the fragments of bone and bullet, and the wound will heal. if not, it will continue to drain, and in 3 weeks he would have to have surgery to remove the multitudes of fragments.

when i first got to the vet's, she took me back to show me all big dog's x-rays, and go over the dog's status. while he had not been badly treated, he was riddled with parasites, and not that well nourished. and while he is docile and friendly, he shows no indications of really having any training beyond house breaking. big dog is a project.

after we came out of the x-ray room, we walked past the door to the room where the dogs are kept. immediately, i heard a dog start barking loudly.

the vet smiled, and said, "your little boy found his voice." i didn't realize it was big dog barking, because i hadn't heard him bark before. more seriously, she told me that this breed is very owner attached. apparently big dog thinks he is mine.

thank god for his gentle nature, because he does not like going in the crate. so far it has been a struggle to get him back inside, after each time i let him out.

considering how i have wrestled him tonite, it is rather funny how nervous i was about pushing him into the car yesterday. i haven't yet figured out what i am going to do about him when i go to work tomorrow. he might have to be chained instead of crated...altho he might be able to snap any chain i have right now.

do any of you listers need a good dog project? i already have one needy dog, in the little dog, and i don't see how i can do justice to the big dog, too.

laz

may 20, 2010
last update on the big dog

big dog is not loving this crate deal.
he balks at going in, and sometimes he barks away wanting out.
but it is truly the only way to enforce rest on his injured leg.

he did get to be out yesterday afternoon as my poor daughter
had to let him out for his mid-day potty break and she was not
able to get him back inside. so he got to spend a few hours on a
chain instead. if that happens again today, it wont be the worst
thing in the world.

i know that when i got out of my car yesterday afternoon
he was the happiest dog on earth.
(even if i did eventually put him back in the crate)

i have come to realize that, incredible as it seems,
this dog was raised indoors.
his desire to go in the house is only a clue.
the dead giveaway was last night.
i was taking him on one of his little walks
when a toad hopped in front of him.
he pounced and picked it up in his mouth.

he spat it right back out,
but i have NEVER seen a dog pick up the second toad they ever
saw.

now i realize just how terrified he must have been the first time i
saw him. and how clueless he was about what to do outdoors.
the poor creature was going up to anyone he saw, to beg for help.
all we saw was the visage of a demon,
and we yelled, threw rocks, or shot at him.

now for his status:

he waited for his food this morning.
he did come able to obey the command to sit when he arrived.
but he was used to rushing his food or water.

17

i was comfortable enough this morning to make him sit
while i held his food bowl.
then to withdraw it when he tried to jump at it as i set it down.
after a few tries he finally sat long enough for me to set the bowl
down...
his "wait" after that was about 2 seconds, but we are on the way.
then i put my hand on him while he ate (a couple of light pats)
which he accepted without any reaction.

he is getting a little easier to put into the crate.
he has probably been crated as punishment in the past,
so this will take some extra time.
but we are getting there.

he is getting the idea that i will tell him where to do his business,
and getting to where he can be walked on the leash without
brute force.
this is a very trainable dog.

as you would wish from a dog, his idea of a great reward is to be
petted and told how good he is. for my part, when i look into
those green/yellow eyes, i no longer see the devil. i see affection
and trust. we have both grown in the last 6 days.

as for his wound. he is still a tripod when he moves. but he is
putting the bad leg's foot on the ground when he stands.
let me admit, at this time, it has been funny to watch him pee.
when he hikes a back leg, he cannot balance on the two
remaining legs. so he leans against the tree while he pees.
(i know the feeling, big dog. ya gotta do what ya gotta do!)
this morning, however, he used the bad foot to stabilize his food
bowl. this is huge, since nerve damage was the big question
mark. that is a pretty complex task and gives real hope that he
will eventually have a complete recovery. i hope he does, because
prior to the injury he was poetry in motion.

i have had several requests to see pictures. so i got chrys to take
some pictures with her cell phone yesterday. i just don't know
how to get them posted where list people could see them.
(and i know y'all want to see how pretty my baby boy is).

i think some of you do that facebook thing with chrys (or that is what she tells me). maybe you could tell her how to put the pictures up?

now for the ultra part.
i see posts on this list all the time about running dogs.
well, i know where a person could get a fabulous running partner for absolutely no cash outlay (other than the trip to get him).
he has had all his shots, and all that other stuff taken care of.
he has a proven good disposition, good behavior around people and other dogs, and is at the very beginning stages of being trained.
i have developed a genuine fondness for this animal in a short period of time, but am under a lot of pressure to find him a new home (back me up here, case. tell them what kind of pressure i am under). i won't give him to someone unless i think they are capable of doing right by him, because he is a huge and powerful animal and if he is not properly trained...well, look what happened with his first owner.

i just don't know for sure what to do if i can't find big dog a home. if i had a fenced in yard for him it would be different, but i can't no way afford that. i cannot let him run free, he would just get shot again. i have my doubts about teaching him to stay at home without a fence or chain, because he didn't get the early start little dog got and no dog should ever spend most of their life on a chain. i have to believe that someone on this list needs a big dog to run with?

laz

may 22, 2010
big dog pictures

i am not sure why he was so scary when he came running up to my car a week ago today. in these pictures i just see a big baby who wants to be cuddled...

we put him in front of a shetland pony for scale in the standing photo.

progress report on his leg:

he still carries it half the time, but half the time he walks on it with a pronounced limp.

and training:

he is getting the idea about walking without pulling, tho he needs plenty more work and josh didn't tell me what to do about a dog who salivates like victoria falls while waiting permission to eat! what a fantastic running dog he could be...

you better hurry while we can still stand to be parted.

laz

may 26, 2010
big dog's clock

i worry about the big dog.

he had a prospective permanent home earlier.
but that fell thru.

so the ultralist dog continues towards an uncertain future.

as his leg keeps healing,
the challenges of big dog grow.

for one thing, he is part houdini.
he can pop latches with his nose,
wiggle apart loose connections with his paw,
and in a pinch, apply brute force with his shoulder.

he has approached each crate and chain
with the measured professional calm of a military sapper,
studying, calculating, and testing
before implementing the latest plan in his devious mind.
i have come to dread the words, "big dog is out."

altho there is a secret grin
every time big dog proves his mastery over another cage
or confinement.
because the only thing he wants to get free for, is to join me.

at the moment,
the new cage that i big-dog proofed with a pair of vise-grips
holds the edge on big dog.
he appears to be accepting it calmly
but i can't help think something is perking in that broad head.

he is learning his craft at being an owned dog.
waiting for his signal to eat
doing his business in appropriate places
and walking on a leash.

he slips up now and then with the tricky stuff
and when he really wants to go where we are walking to,
he is like walking a john deere tractor.
sooner beats later, if you are a big dog.

but most of all, he is just a big sweet baby.
he never tires of his favorite thing;
leaning his massive head against my leg,
while receiving various rubs, strokes, and pats.

i don't think he knows that,
while i am stroking that broad head
(chrys commented, "i can put my hand flat on top of his head,
and my fingers don't reach over the sides!")
and looking into those trusting eyes,
i am worried about big dog.

this is not a permanent solution for big.
i already have a special needs dog,
and by the time his leg is completely healed
big dog is going to need to be out a lot more.
he will need someone to make him a working dog
or a running dog...

and my running dog job is more than adequately filled.

i know there must be a place for big dog.
his path cannot have brought him here
only to see him end his days prematurely,
because no one has a place for him.
it is so unfair for a dog with so much to give.
someone must need this gentle giant.

but big dog's clock is ticking.

laz

may 29, 2010
big dog gets a job

as i write this, i can look out the window and see big dog stretched out, enjoying the luxury of a 20x10 kennel.
for this he wants the listers to know how grateful he is.
the generosity of listers paid his medical bills, and there was enough left over to provide him a 10x10 kennel now that he is getting around a lot better.

i figured that he deserved a bigger space than that, and decided there were probably some luxuries i could do without, so we got the extra panels to make it 10x20.

ok, he is not exactly enjoying it, because what big dog wants is to come in the house.
but he would settle for freedom.

of course, during the last week he has tasted freedom a time or two. he finally defeated the latest crate, after nearly two days.
of course, i had done considerable alterations to fortify it against all of big-dog's known angles of attack,
but the big dog showed why he has been adopted by the list.
like any good ultrarunner, he simply never gives up. he is tough, determined, and crafty. secretly watching him thru the window, it was fascinating to see him simply sit and stare at the cage.
he studied and studied, you could almost see the wheels turning inside that massive head. then, every so often, he would take his nose,or his paw, or his shoulder, and test something.
when he finally detected a weakness, he was relentless.
attacking and attacking, until the next thing i knew he was at the back door, peering in and wagging his tail.

i hardened the crate further.
he took another day to defeat it again.

then he snapped his chain. the same one he had managed to detatch several times previously.

so, while i was constructing another crate
(from the ample supply of crate parts i now have)
big dog decided it was time to do some exploring
and took off running down the hill.
my worries about big dog being able to run were unfounded.
he is still walking with a limp, but he can once again run with the
fluid grace of a big cat.
god, what a beautiful animal.

i hollered at him that he better come back if he didn't want to
end up shot again.
he just stopped and looked back at me.
(i am pretty sure he was grinning)
then he went on down the hill.
i threatened to just let him go, but i was lying.
i went down and found him playing in the front yard of the little
house.
when i called he just looked at me and grinned.
when i went closer, he moved further off, and grinned at me
again.

after a few minutes of cat and mouse, i finally told him,
"ok, you silly fool. whatever happens is on you."

i turned and started back for the house.

big dog followed.
when i turned to look at him, he came on up and let me put his
leash on again.
his laughing eyes said he was just having a little fun.

however, i knew it was time to get him out of the crate.
he was well enough to be needing more space, and the burden of
getting up extra early, and coming home from work in the middle
of the day, etc, to tend to him was wearing me out.

so i counted out the remainder of the "big dog money" $245.
i did not think it would be enough for a kennel, but i called
around anyway. i finally found one at the co-op that was cheap
enough. a 10x10 kennel was only $252!

a 20x10 was $378. twice the space seemed more than reasonable for such a big dog, so i bought it. (please, nobody tell on me!) unfortunately, my truck didn't start (it isn't always great to drive a 50 year old truck) so i had to beg a friend to go with me to pick up the kennel. big dog is lucky so many people are willing to help him out. after half constructing the thing when i got home, i discovered that the idiot kids working at the co-op had packed me a kennel with a defective door, and one broken clamp.

the door could have waited until i had a working vehicle to get a replacement panel. but there was no point trying to confine big dog in a kennel with a missing clamp. albert pupenstein would spot that weakness so fast, he would probably beat me back to the house after i put him in his pen.

i couldn't carry the whole panel without a truck, so i removed only the door, and tied it on top of my car, to race back to town before closing time.
there, two of the goofy kids took my defective door to replace it, while the third got me a new clamp.
i pointed out that the new clamp was twice the size of the old one, and asked that he locate one the same size, so it would work.
by the time he found one that was about the right size, his buddies had returned with my replacement door.
a smarter man would have asked if they replaced my door with another door of the same size. but this man did not think of that until he replaced the door in the panel, and found that it was so small the latch wouldn't reach.

tomorrow i call the co-op and tell them they owe me a new door panel. i am tempted to tell them i have a big dog smarter than all three of their stockroom workers combined, and that dog needs a job.

meanwhile, that clever big dog is laying there studying the new prison, especially the jerry-rigged door that is holding him in. i expect his smiling face to be at the back door at any moment.

free to a good home...
one canine genius (with a sense of humor)
laz

may 30, 2010
big dog and the invisible fence

i considered two things & decided against the invisible fence...

1) owners of large dogs gave the fences mixed reviews
(altho i heard one darn funny story about a fence being jacked up
until a great dane had sparks jumping off his testicles - i don't
want to fry little dog in order to make big dog shake his head in
dismay!).
given big dog's size, imperviousness to pain, determination and
cleverness, i was dubious about the effectivity of the fence.

2) i live in the woods... literally... to dig a trench around my
house, even a shallow trench, thru all the rocks and roots, would
be a monumental undertaking.

by the way:
big dog escaped the new kennel twice yesterday despite my best
efforts to jerry-rig the door.
so i moved him back to the resurrected crate,
which he demolished by the end of the afternoon.

he is now an expert on the weaknesses of metal crates... first you
gotta remove the clamps that "god" fastens around the borders of
the different panels, then you find a place where you can get two
panels to separate a little bit...
while he was destroying the crate, i was buying a cable to fasten
him back inside the kennel.
when i left the house this morning, big was attached to a tree by
the cable, inside the kennel. i am not making any bets on where
he is right now!

laz (smarter than the AVERAGE dog, but apparently not smarter
than EVERY dog)

june 02, 2010
big dog wins again

it was the ultimate in canine containment.
a chain link fence taller than my head.
2 inch pipes bracing it.
the base buried in the ground
with big boulders against the bottom...
inside & out.

it looked so impressive.
sort of a puppy gulag.

except for the gaping hole in the side.
with a big red dog sitting next to it.

the big dog had to sit next to it.
he only had about a foot of his cable left.
there was barely enough for him to get outside the fence and sit.

he figured out how to unravel chain link fence in only two days.

but the braided steel cable.
he hasn't figured out how to defeat that one yet.
he did get the fastener unlatched once.
however, i saw him coming out,
and caught him before he could get out of the yard.

he might have gotten it open that once,
but it has this challenging fastener
that i struggle to open with two hands (and instructions)
he had to have just gotten lucky.

none the less, i have hidden it from him just to be safe.

anyway,
here is this dog.
seems to have gotten himself thru the fence,
and then got his cable snagged.
because he is jumping and barking.

the cable is too short,
and pulling his head down.
he looks terribly uncomfortable.

i go over and free him and he is overjoyed.
of course, he is always overjoyed.

after i feed and water him, we spend about 30 minutes working.
then i return him to the pen & hook him to his cable.

as i walk towards the house,
he goes straight to the hole,
squeezes thru it & stands there
with the short cable pulling his head down.

idiot.

there he sits. barely enough room to move.
i suppose in a little while i will have to go and free him again.
if i can come up with a way to close the hole.

a little while later, i am in the house
and i catch a glimpse of movement outside.
peeking around the corner of the window
so big can't see me
i see him easily slip back thru the hole,
walk across his pen,
and get a big drink of water.

then he walked calmly back across
crawled back out the hole
and took up his position of visible torment.
i am pretty sure that when i walked into sight
he stuck his tongue out a little further
and bugged his eyes out more just for effect.

this dog is an evil genius.

chrys just calls him houdini.

laz

32

june 15, 2010
the big and little war

it is the fearless little who has become big's real playmate.
little is unfazed by big's size, but i find it difficult to watch when
they play their game. the first time i saw them, i had to remind
myself that they had been playing all along, and little had yet to
be injured.

i was out in the yard, doing some yard work.
little was out with me and had been in and out of big's pen all
morning.
the sound of the two playing was disturbing enough.
all the snarling and growling and crashing around sounded like a
dog war was going on.

i happened to walk by as the two were going at it, and there they
were, standing on their hind legs and meeting in what appeared
to be mortal combat right in the center of the pen.
being the larger dog, big was pushing little back.
big was also skilled at using his bulk to bang little around when
they were on the ground, the same way he had used his shoulder
to knock little off the porch when little had the gall to try to steal
big's food.
with a couple of quick moves, big knocked little onto her back,
and in a flash he was on top, pinning the smaller dog on her back
with her entire neck engulfed in his massive jaws.

my first instinct was that i should separate them, but i had seen
big bite a cow leg-bone in two, just to eat the marrow.
if he bit down, little would be a goner before i could move.
so i just turned my head and looked away.
i didn't want to see little die.
i made a mental note that i could not let little play with big any
more.
one careless moment and he might kill my little.

the snarling and crashing around continued...
and then i heard little's distinctive high pitched war cry.
curiosity overcame my better judgement,

33

so i peeked back....
and there was big, flat on his back with all four legs in the air.
little was standing on his chest and had big by the throat!
big looked over at me, his eyes twinkling with merriment.
his mouth was wide open and he appeared to be laughing.

all i could do was to laugh with him.
big knows how to make a joke

i erased my mental note.
little is in good hands... or is that paws?

laz

june 29, 2010
big sunrise

i "overslept" this morning.
usually big wakes me up before 5 am,
barking his, "IT IS TIME TO WORK!!!!" bark.

big loves his morning workout.
but he was up late last night.
anything past sunset is late as far as big is concerned,
because he needs to get up before sunrise
to be ready for his morning routine.

last night he had a visitor:
sam, whose brother tony is soon to be big's new number one.
it is a long drive to st louis,
and sam wanted big to be familiar with the person taking him.

i know this is the best thing for big.
tony is a young guy,
former college football player,
a responsible, experienced dog-owner
newly out on his own, with a lot of outdoor activities going on
and a desire for a big dog for a companion.

sam sat in (or walked along)
while big went thru his routine yesterday afternoon.
that way tony can pick up with the things big knows how to do
and the commands that he understands.
continuity will be good for big.
big must have thought it was an important test,
because he performed like a champ yesterday.

he even did a near perfect job walking,
which he has had trouble with in the past
when there were distracting strangers around.

anyway, big and i got off to slightly late start this morning.
big was being unusually quiet and calm.
as with most mornings, i talked and big listened.

35

this morning we talked about how happy big was going to be.
about the big fenced in yard he was going to have
and all the neat trails he was going to get to explore
with his new number one.
i even let it slip that he would be getting to sleep inside!!!

big just focused on matching my pace exactly
head beside my knee, shoulders not passing my legs.

i told big how much i had enjoyed working with him;
watching him progress from an uneducated dog
who dimly remembered how to sit from his puppy days
and was like walking a john deere tractor,
to an accomplished dog, with a repertoire of skills.
big looked straight ahead and stayed on task.
i wondered what thoughts were passing thru that massive head.

we passed the curve where the rabbits play.
usually big has to be reminded of his duties there
as he wants to sniff about,
and maybe pursue a rodent into the briars.

we passed all the places we usually turn around
but big was doing so well, we just kept going.
finally we came out atop a small rise.
ahead of us spread miles of forests and fields
light mists rising here and there.
in the distance a line of wooded hills
stretched across the entire horizon.
the pink glow of a perfect sunrise tinted the sky around the
tiniest speck of red sun just peeking over the center hill.

big and i stopped to watch in silence.
big usually takes stops as an opportunity to snuffle about in the
bushes.
this morning he stood solemnly beside me, watching the sun
come up.

"you know, don't you big? somehow you know."
big just looked up at me.
then he leaned his enormous head against my leg to be petted.

36

i obliged, while feeling tears well up in my eyes.
i was not sure i could talk, so i said nothing.

all too soon, the sun was above the horizon,
and it was time for me & big to head for the house.

we walked back, each lost in our own thoughts.
i was imagining waking up
and not having big moaning with pleasure
when i came out of the house with his blue leash.

i was picturing the hole in my heart
without his thousand funny tricks
and that silly grin to greet me every time i came home.

i was thinking about him leaping as high as my head with joy
as i came walking across the yard
and then forcing himself to sit
("you don't get petted 'til you are under control")
perfectly still, except fairly vibrating with excitement.

i thought about my gentle giant
and the frightening play-fighting between him and little dog
and his marvelous abilty to play such rough games
without ever hurting his diminutive friend.

big's thoughts, he kept to himself.
but i think they were happy thoughts.

big is a special dog,
and he deserves the so-much-more that tony can give him.
he needs someone young and strong, like big himself,
someone who can let him use that incredible athleticism.
someone who can keep up.

but, god, i am going to miss him so.

doing the right thing is not always easy.

laz

june 30, 2010
countdown

tony has been warned. the dog he is adopting channels houdini.

he plans to start with big on a cable *and* inside the fenced in yard.

i wish him luck!

for my part,
i just hope big don't manage to get his-self shot today.
tomorrow morning he goes to the vet to be neutered, and the
next morning sam will pick him up to start his trek to the
gateway city. i just need to get big thru one last day alive.

the scoundrel has escaped 3 times just in the past week, the last
one being yesterday. allison (from the farm behind mine) called
to say that big & little had come over to visit.
(and that she had put her dogs up out of fear of big).

big and little had returned home by the time i got there.
big and little are quite a pair
(little is going to miss him an awful lot).
they have become inseparable,
but neither is a good influence on the other.

part of me admires that wily dog for his intelligence and
determination,
but the rest of me fears the possible consequences of his
proclivity for escape. dogs like big are targets when they are
loose.

oh well. i did the best i could; tightening his collar, reinforcing his
attachments, and replacing the bright white tick collar he had
managed to remove during the night.

the hope is that seeing that white collar might discourage a
shooter, should big find another way to escape today.
but his best protection is that i know i wont have to work late
today.

how can you blame him for yesterday. he waited patiently until it
was time for his walk, and when i didn't show, he walked himself.
so big and i have a walk this evening, a walk in the morning,
and then he goes to the vet.

i will go by the vets again when they take him out in the
afternoon/evening...
to pet him and let him know he isn't abandoned,
and then i will meet sam there the next morning to help her load
him up and say my farewells.

i would like to bring him home for his last night.
but there is no way i could keep him contained,
and away from little,
as his surgery calls for.
big is an irresistable force.

i have a promise that, when tony goes to georgia to visit family,
he and big will stop by on the way...
at least as long as big remembers who i am.

and i have a promise of updates and pictures for the list.
i had to inform tony that his new dog has a fan club.

that is not exactly what you expect to hear about a rescue dog,
but big is far from your average rescue dog.

(word is, after they made big they killed the mold maker)

laz

part 2: abandoned

big loneliness

hello, my name is big.
i am a very sad dog.
i have no master.
i have no important work to do.
i am so very lonely.

it was not always this way.
i have had many masters.
but no one wants to keep me.
i am not a good enough dog.

i had a mean master.
he was not nice to me, but he was my master.
i tried to be a good dog
but he took me out into the woods and left me.

then i had a kind master.
he rescued me when i was hurt and frightened.
he gave me important work to do.
it was a very happy time.
then one day he sent me away.
he got into a truck with me,
then he left me inside and another man drove away with me.
i watched the kind master until i could see him no more.
i was afraid i would never see him again.
that is what happens if i am not a good enough dog.

i was passed from one person to another.
i went for many long rides in different cars.
i knew i was far from my home in the woods
and far from the kind master.
then i came to a new master, the young master.

i was very happy with the young master.
there was only him and me.
i had a schedule.
he gave me lots of important work to do.
i got to sleep in his bed and live in his house.

then we moved to a new place.
there were many young men
and the young master did not have so much time for me.
i had no schedule
and i had no important work to do.
but i had the young master.
so i was happy.

one day young master took me for a long ride.
we came to a place with people i knew from before.
young master told me goodbye
and i knew i was going to be alone again.
this has happened to me before.
i watched for him to come back for a long time.
but he never came back.
i had not been a good enough dog.

now i am very sad.
there are people in my house.
i get plenty to eat.
but i have no master of my own.
no one pets me.
no one gives me important work to do.
every day i sit on a chain in the yard
and i am lonely.
sometimes children gather and throw rocks at me,
and i cannot run away.
i am a very sad dog.

big dog

july 03, 2010
if you see a big red dog grinning out a car window

if there has ever been a community owned dog, it is big.
he owes his life to the kindness of the listers.

big started his journey to his new home yesterday.

he began his new life at the same place he started his tenure as
the list dog, at the vet's office.
however, this was a very different big than the one at that first
visit.
the old big was nervous around strangers
eyeing all those odd people and dogs suspiciously.
for their part, those people looked at big with a tinge of fear,
and pulled their own pets closer.

thanks in good part to the many runners & listers who passed by
the house during big's time, he was a transformed dog this visit.
i had dropped him off to get neutered on thursday,
and went to get him an hour before his ride was to show up
so we could have one last visit.

we went out under some shade trees next to the vet's office to
spend our last hour and big was like a superstar.
every time someone arrived, he treated them to that giant happy
grin, and wagged his tail. as if drawn by a magnet, nearly every
one of them came over and petted his monstrous head.
big fairly beamed with pleasure.
several of them had dogs, which they unconcernedly allowed to
approach big. big just wagged his tail even harder, and sniffed
noses. even with a chubby little chihuahua that he could have
swallowed whole.

the training worked. big had seen all kinds of strangers. women,
men, men in hats, men with umbrellas, men in big coats, you
name it. and a lot of those people were y'all coming to visit big.
likewise, his exposure to lots of strange dogs.
big had learned to look forward to visits from strangers, and
acted like every person coming up was his long-lost best friend.

45

too soon it was time to load him up in the truck to head off.
big was not too anxious to get in the strange vehicle, and after we
managed to get him into the front floorboard, i tricked my hairy
friend one last time.

i went and opened the passenger door and called him over. he
jumped right in, thinking he was going to be with me.
i watched big drive away with a heavy heart, then i went to work.

last night i got an update.
there was a picture of big sitting in the truck, looking out the
passenger window with that ear to ear grin on his face.
big likes riding in the car, and unlike my car, the passenger
window on the truck works. instead of sniffing the vent, he got to
stick his head out the window!

big had then spent the afternoon with sam and her dog fiddy.
at the time they sent the picture, sam and fiddy were playing
fetch.

big was following fiddy out, watching her pick up the ball, and
then following her back. he was, apparently, enjoying the game
immensely.

later on i got one final message. sam, fiddy, and big were curled
up on the couch watching tv.
sam said there was one small problem. she didn't want to give
big up tomorrow (today now). i know just how she feels.

so big will be arriving at his permanent home in a few hours. he
will come with a clean bill of health, a collar, a leash, a crate
(the least destroyed of his several crates),
a food bowl and a big sack of food, a cable, a good start on
training, his own dog-training consultant, and $117.
for a rescue dog, big is a wealthy dog.

and this whole happy ending is all thanks to y'all on the list.
when big arrived, i started into this adventure with the best of
intentions.
but i could have never covered all his medical bills, and
incidental expenses.

46

i have a farm. and one can have either a farm or money. one does not get to have both. if it were not for the unsolicited donations of the list, big would have had to been turned over to animal control. even those who offered only moral support, it meant a lot.

so all of y'all out there. feel good today. tony and big are going to have a great life together, and y'all made it possible.

and if you happen to be driving between nashville and st louis today, and you see a big, red dog grinning out a car window at you, give him a wave and smile back. that will be big dog, and he just wants to say thanks.

laz

july 4, 2010
if you are not a licensed vet...

then you should not remove stitches.

big dog (now residing in st louis) failed to follow this advice.
apparently, he noticed the embroidery on his scrotum,
and (altho they realized what he was about to do)
no one was quick enough to stop him from removing the stitches.

there was quite a bit of blood
and the remainder of big's purse went to yet another vet bill!

i received a great picture of a huge dog wearing a diaper and a
cone the size of a garbage can...

he looked a little sheepish.

and another big dog story:
when the vet STAPLED HIS SCROTUM,
big dog wriggled loose from those holding him.

if i was that vet, i'd have probably lost 10 years off my life
because big went straight for his face...

and licked him.

now *that* is a friendly dog.

laz

july 10, 2010
big genius

i apologize for having forgotten to pass along the update on the
big dog in his new home...

tony is finding out what we all already know.
big is a friendly fella, but he has his own mind.
and he is a dog genius.

now that he is an inside dog,
big had to get used to waiting to go outside.
not that much of a problem for big,
he never wanted to go in his pen.
(he just bit a hole thru the chain link fence & went outside to go!)
we figured he would probably not have a much trouble adapting
to not going in a house.

he did "mark" a couple of chairs that first afternoon...which
would be like spraying them with a 1-liter bottle of mello yello
(big doesn't have any "weak flow" issues)
however, they yelled "no" at him a both times,
and he never went inside again.

on the other hand, when big was spotted drinking from the toilet,
the new master put the lid down.
big just put it back up and got another drink
(i can almost see the laughter in his eyes)

likewise, poor hopeful tony failed to appreciate the deeper
meaning of the dis-assembled crate that came with big.
he went out and got a new crate (meant to contain giant dogs).

the first time he had to leave big for a few hours,
he put big in the crate in a bedroom, and shut the door.

when he got home, the crate was in two pieces, the bedroom
door was open (altho not damaged?) and big was waiting by the
back door.

tony decided big might as well be left out when he was gone.

i don't think i will ever see pit bulls the same way again.
they didn't used to make me laugh.

laz

august 23, 2010
the latest on big dog

i heard from tony today.
he and big have moved into a frat-house (?!)

good old big has adapted with aplomb.
working the room like a pro,
collecting petting and attention all day long.
during parties, he takes up a station under a table,
and just watches the goings on.

he also has a mini pack of 5 dogs he spends time with.
the other dogs cavort & play,
while big just stands amidst them and watches
with that big grin on his face.

lastly, he likes to go to the river with everyone.
he enjoys swimming with them,
but has a particular soft spot for lying on a log in the sun.

thanks to the ultra-list community,
this is one happy dog!

i inquired about the possiblity of big making a guest appearance
at the backyard ultra, but havent heard anything yet.

laz (wishing he could have a big hug)

december 25, 2001
the big hole in my heart

i keep reminding myself that he was only a dog.
on top of that, he was only here for two months.

but i still miss the big fella.

i miss him barking to tell me it is time for our walk.
i miss him doing flips when i come home.
i miss the laughter in his eyes when he has played a good joke on
me and the look of joy on his ugly face when someone pets him.
i even miss chasing him down after his latest amazing escape.

i had hoped tony would stop by with him over the Christmas
holidays but that didn't happen.
sometimes i wonder if the big dog remembers his house in the
woods.
or have we faded from memory as he enjoys his good new life.

i know i did the right thing.
but when the big dog left,
he left a big hole in my heart.

laz

february 27, 2011
big again??

amy came home the other night with disturbing news.
she had gone to nashville to visit friends,
only to find that big dog was there.
new master tony had to find somewhere for him to stay
while he finished the semester...
because big got thrown out of his current housing.

big is a very sad dog,
because all the people in the house have their own dogs,
and big now has no master.
and big's hearts desire is to belong to somcone.

the problem is, big has lost his training.
when amy arrived she was nearly knocked down
when big jumped up on her.
she was totally unprepared, because it was big.

last time she saw him, he was a perfect gentleman.
now he is just an enormous unruly dog.
a really friendly enormous dog, but unruly.

so i have been asked to restore the big of old.
it took a lot of begging
(and a healthy dose of telling how sad big was,
and what a hard life he has had)
but i have permission for big to stay for two months.

of course, i made demands.
he has to come with an igloo doghouse, and a 30 foot cable.
i already know he can simply bite a hole thru the chain link fence
of my current pen.

i am hoping the training isn't buried too deep.
last time i got to start with a big who'd been shot
and was nearly dead.

this time, i will have a full strength big.

he isn't here, yet.
so it isn't a sure thing.
but i don't think the current guardians are too amused by his cleverness.
last i heard, he had decided to use the cat door...

did i say *cat* door?
i think it is a *big dog* door, now.

laz

part 3: homecoming

big is home

hello. my name is big.
and i am a very lucky dog.
i have come home.

i was living on a chain in the yard.
there was a man who fed me,
but he did not want to be my master.
no one had work for me to do.
no one petted me.
no one told me i was a good dog.
it was not a happy time.

but one day the man took me for a long ride.
i was worried
because long rides always mean my life is going to change.

every time we stopped i looked around to see where we were.
when we stopped the last time i knew where we were
we were at the house in the woods
this is where the kind master lives.

my tail started wagging when i saw the house.
it wagged harder when we got out.
i ran to the door as fast as i could go,
and the kind master was there.

now it is like i was never gone.
i have my own house.
i have a schedule.
i have important work to do.
there are many rules for me to remember but i try very hard,
and master always tells me what a good dog i am.

every day is a new adventure,
filled with surprises.
i am a very lucky dog.

big dog

march 18, 2011
the bigloo

the bigloo barely touched the ground
before big was inside, looking contentedly out
that big smile splitting his big head nearly in two.
big loves his bigloo...

but the bigloo story doesn't begin there.

when big first got to st louis, he was something of a celebrity.
armed with good manners he was the consumate party animal,
working the crowd like a pro.
every human encounter ended the same;
his big ugly head leaned against someone's leg
a look of ecstacy on his big ugly face while "someone" petted him.

big got to go everywhere.
strolling around campus, hiking in the woods,
and his favorite; swimming at the lake,
where he swam out to a big log, climbed up
and lay there in the sun, watching his people play in the water.

but big dogs are not born with manners.
big was born with a sweet puppy heart, the face of a devil,
and the strength of 10 dogs.
manners he had to learn, and his lessons were not kept up.

big slowly turned from a campus celebrity to a campus terror.
and one day he found himself campus banished.

tony & big came to visit tony's sister one weekend,
and when the weekend ended,
he informed her that big was staying...
just 'til the end of the semester.

big's time in nashville was not his happiest time.
amy came home & told me about big's plight.
she said, "i went in and there was big.
i said 'BIG!' and then i was down on the floor.

i wasn't ready for big to jump up on me...
i mean, it was big.
he knows better than that. or he used to."

big created havoc in his new home.
he stole food and destroyed everything in sight when he was
inside. he barked continuously when he was outside.

if no one was watching, he raided the refrigerator.
attempts to walk him amounted to being dragged down the
street to wherever big wanted to go.
neighbors were terrified of him.
big was not a welcome guest.

amy said, "i feel so sorry for him.
he just goes from person to person looking for attention
and everyone pushes him away.
the more they ignore him, the worse he acts.
big *needs* his person."

you guys know how this ended.
a week ago last tuesday there was a knock at the door.
outside was arthur... and big.
big was wagging his tail a mile a minute.
i opened the door, leaned over, & big was in my arms in a flash
arthur said, "he sure remembers this place.
he's been wagging his tail since we got out of the truck."

big was ready to go to his old home, the pen.
but amy's dog, sophie, uses the pen, now.
(i don't know where amy gets these strange names for her pets)
and the holes big would bite thru the chain link
(for his convenience)
wouldn't work with sophie.
we had repaired the pen,
and didn't need big to customize it again.

as we went by his pen,
he seemed surprised that his west side hole was not there
and he reached out to bite a new one.
"no, big, you aren't staying there. you have a new place."

64

i took him out to where we had him one of those igloo doghouses
full of straw. big stuck his head in the door & looked around.
then the rest of him followed.
he turned around to stick his head out the door,
a huge grin splitting his face. big was home.

in the days since, big has fallen easily into his old routines.
he greets me by jumping higher than my head and doing flips.
but he has relearned not jumping on me.
he got past the towing mode of walking in about 50 feet.
at first he thought he was supposed to snatch his food.
now, he turns his head to watch me while he waits on permission
to eat.
i can see his yellow/green eyes glowing with big dog worship.
bit by bit, we are relearning how to act,
and big is loving every minute.

in the mornings, little gets to work first,
and big waits patiently.
but, when me & little
take the first step on the driveway coming back
(1/4 mile from the house)
big starts barking & carrying on.
if dog workouts are late, big lets me know.
there is a schedule to keep,
and big has important work to do.

big seems to be a contented dog, now.
he loves to lay in the sun,
he loves to prance about,
he loves to work,
but (most of all)
big loves to sit safe & secure in his bigloo, looking out.

unfortunately, altho the bigloo was the biggest they make
it was not the sturdiest.
it wasn't made with big in mind.
plastic slots and pins have short life expectancy with this huge
block of muscle going in and out.
the 5 screws (for added strength) were a joke.
the bigloo was reduced to rubble in a little over a week.

so last night, i took the bigloo and rebuilt it,
attaching the pieces with "plastic weld"
poor big was relegated to sleeping outside on a pile of straw
while the toxic smelling bigloo cured & aired out.

after he did his work this morning,
i brought his bigloo back.
and that is where we began.
can the reinforced bigloo stand up to the big now?
we will soon find out.
if not, we will just have to find another solution.

well, i gotta go.
i think there are a big & a little waiting for me.
they are training me for an attempt at the strolling jim
(a 40 mile race)

laz

march 21, 2011
death of the bigloo

well, we found out what was happening to the bigloo.
amy was watching out the window...

big has a tarp hung up,
so he has a place out of the rain without being in his bigloo.
big pushed the bigloo out from under the tarp,
then tried to climb on it, so he could see what was on top of the
tarp.

yes, i know dogs can't think like that.
but someone forgot to tell big.

the bigloo, meanwhile, is about half demolished again.
i think i need to get a lot more epoxy this time...
or figure a way to fasten the bigloo down permanently in one
place.

laz

april 12, 2011
what's up with big?

what is the deal with big?
how did such an ugly beast come to have a fan club?

maybe it is about big's difficult life.
being abandoned, shot, rescued, and abandoned again.

maybe it is about big's resilient good nature.
a dog that never bears a grudge or feels sorry for himself,
a dog that loves everyone and cannot understand why they
would not love him.

maybe it is about me & big's destiny to be together.
three times, big has been sent away... supposedly to a better life.
three times he has returned in need of a friend.

i had hoped to take big to barkley,
but his retraining just had not progressed far enough.
not that i thought big presented a threat to anyone,
but he is still a feared pit bull.
his manners have to be impeccable...
especially to be around the general public at a park campground.

so, arthur agreed to board big over barkley weekend.
big greeted arthur with joy.
big loves arthur.
and he hopped in arthur's truck without hesitation.
big loves to go for rides.

big didn't know this ride would take him away for nearly a week!

when arthur brought big back,
big was hopping around in the truck,
wagging his tail and moaning with joy.
as soon as arthur attached the leash,
big was out of the truck & off.
arthur might as well have been walking a john deere tractor
as big made a beeline around the house to his bigloo...

dragging arthur behind him.
there he sat down and waited for his cable to be attached.
big was home, and meant to stay there.

now we are back on our schedule.
we walk between 04:00 and 04:30,
so big "reminds" me it is about time if i don't show up by 04:15.

big keeps careful track of the schedule
(he must have a PDA in the bigloo)
he knows when it is time for walking,
time to eat,
and time for his bed check.
and he is prepared to remind me, if i forget...

yet, sunday morning, when i was not at home,
big slept in & didn't bark.

big doesn't just bark and bark for the sake of barking.
he barks to communicate.
and you don't have to wonder what he is barking about.
big's barks are very distinct.

he has his greeting bark.
the bigloo being out of sight of the driveway,
big could easily miss greeting each new arrival,
and that is one of his important jobs.
so, when someone arrives at the house,
big gives his greeting bark
so they will come around and tell him hello.
(a pat or two is also appreciated)
once he has greeted each person,
he turns and retires to his bigloo.

he has his timer bark.
this means something has come up on the schedule,
and i am late!!!

he has a special bark for answering dogs on other farms.
this is his lowest possible bark.

and he has his "help me" bark.
this is his highest pitched bark.
it even sounds desperate.
for some reason, big thinks i can fix anything.

last night was a stormy night in middle tennessee,
with heavy rain and high winds.
about midnight, i went out to check on big before bed.
i was kind of surprised that the bigloo was still under the tarp.
for that matter, i was half surprised his tarp hadn't blown down.
(altho it has survived numerous previous storms)
i wrote it off to the trees being leafed back out and breaking the
wind.

we had a talk...
big doesn't talk, but he likes to listen to me talking.
like always, big leaned against me contentedly,
while i petted him.
then i told him it was time for bed,
he went in the bigloo.
and i went to the house.

by the time i got ready for bed,
i heard big's "help me" bark.

i looked out the window,
and i could see big standing in the rain at the end of his cable.
that meant he hadn't got tangled.
(big can generally unwind himself if he wraps his cable around a
tree, but once in a while he snags it on a root & needs some help)

i could see the shape of the tarp in the darkness,
so he had a place to get out of the rain.
so i went to bed.
(i am not the best hero a big dog could have)

about every 10 minutes,
all night long,
big would repeat his call for help.
i thought he was just being impatient.
he was going to have to wait for his walk.

finally it came 04:00
and i got up and went out to tell big
we weren't going for a walk, because it was still raining.
there stood big at the end of his cable.
in the rain.
soaking wet.

the top had blown off his bigloo
(must have been right after bed-check)

big commenced making happy sounds & jumping up in the air,
higher than my head.
he was very careful not to jump actually on me,
but his excitement was impossible to contain.
big loves his bigloo.
and big just knew i was going to fix everything.

i dragged the top back over & put it back around the base.
big was so happy, he didn't even seem to mind
when i told him we wouldn't be walking this morning.
(besides, big doesn't like to walk in the rain either)
in lieu of our walk, we had a talk,
and big leaned his soggy head against my leg,
while i patted him and told him i should have paid attention
when he barked last night.
then he went in the bigloo to catch up on his sleep,
while i went in the house.

it has been over a month since big came back for retraining.
as yet, not one call or e-mail from tony to ask how big is doing.

he really ought to remind me every day that big is his dog.

laz

april 14, 2011
like flipping a switch

for a wee bit of ultra content;
big & little have taken me for 12 miles in the last 24 hours
as they continue to train me for the strolling jim.

if i can finish the race, i will have finishes at the same ultra
in the first (1979) and 33rd (2011) editions.

how many people have completed the same ultra over a time
span that long?
possibly ray k at waramaug is the only one i can think of...

now for the continuing story of big dog...

i have always likened owning a dog like big to owning a gun.
while generally harmless, the potential for damage is so great
that it demands an extreme attention paid to safety.

one recurring theme i hear about pit bulls,
that has always worried me,
is that a seemingly gentle & friendly dog
can turn into a vicious killer without warning...
like flipping a switch.

i have told myself that this is not really true,
that people are remarkably unaware of the messages a dog is
sending.
and people really are often unaware.
dogs do not "speak"
but they are very articulate in expressing themselves
with body language and other cues.
that is how they communicate with one another.
dogs are thus well attuned to people's subtle messages,
but we seldom match that with awareness of our dogs.

in the course of exposing big to every possible human encounter,
it has been easy to tell when things make him uncomfortable.
people who are afraid of him make him nervous.

73

and when approached by someone that makes him
uncomfortable, he will back away & give a low growl.
however, he has always been so non-aggressive
that there seemed little chance he would bite
unless he was backed into a corner.
and then it was only a maybe.

in the past week, i have gotten to see the "like flipping a switch"
phenomenon twice.

both involved the buzzards that live in my neighborhood.

big & i were finishing a walk, when amy came up with sophie,
finishing a run. she stopped and was walking in with me,
when we saw buzzards all flocking around one of mr winston's
cows. the cow was trying to chase them off, and we surmised that
it had just had a calf.

buzzards can be dangerous to a newborn calf,
so i held the two dogs while amy went up to tell mr winston
(he would shoot at the buzzards & send them packing)
when amy got to the winston place,
his little border collie type dog came charging out at her
barking & growling like he meant to bite her.

it was like flipping a switch,
big was instantly at the end of his leash,
almost jerking me off my feet.
he didn't growl or bark,
but there was no question of his intentions.

he was going to amy's defense.

it was almost frightening
(the dogs that scare me aren't the ones that bark & growl,
it is the ones that just attack with serious intentions)
big would have snapped that dog in his jaws like a twig.
and he wasn't listening to any verbal commands.

amy came back and big settled down,
but it was an eye opener.

74

yesterday, we experimented with walking all 3 dogs at once.
big has been doing really well
and needed work on more challenging situations.
amy took sophie & little, because they are easy.
i had big.

it started out pretty funny.
big & little are always vying over who is the top dog.
they will play and have a ball,
then little will try some stunt like
putting her front foot on big's shoulder.
big lets her know that wont fly.
that wont stop little from trying some other dominance move
later.
that bullterrier/JRT blood just wont let her give up.

anyway, we walked along with big & little each determined
that they should be the lead dog.
they accept that humans are in charge,
but they were each certain that they were the top dog.
so they were about 2 feet apart,
walking alongside their human as required
with their necks stretched out as far as they could reach,
each trying to get their nose in front.

they never looked directly at each other,
but you could see the whites of their eyes,
as they watched each other out of the corner of their eyes.
good old, no-dominance-issues sophie
walked along the roadside,
focused on snatching blades of grass to eat.

we laughed at our silly dogs,
but it was getting tiresome as they kept pulling out too far,
trying to nose ahead of each other.
so i dropped back about 10 feet
& was in the process of convincing big
that his first responsibility was to walk with me.
amy was watching her two dogs,
and didn't notice as she walked up to a buzzard,
perched on a low branch at about head height.

the buzzard wasn't oblivious.
when amy got about 2 feet away, it took off loudly
(and a buzzard taking flight is *loud*)

little let out a yelp of terror,
and big was off like a shot.
the buzzard flew to a higher branch,
and big was at the end of his leash straining to get loose.
he never took his eyes off the bird that had scared his pack-mate.
he looked like he intended to take it apart, feather by feather.
sophie was still eating grass.
once again, it was like a switch had been flipped.

we walked on a ways, but big & little were too stirred up to
behave so we turned around and took them home.
when we went back past the buzzard roost,
big locked a baleful glare on the buzzard again.
and he kept watching it until we got out of sight.
personally, i don't think even big could have gotten that bird
out of the top of a tree, but i wasn't letting him go to find out.

so there it is.
big is a sweet and gentle dog.
he loves people, and can play & roughhouse with dogs a fraction
his size and never harm a hair on their heads.
he is totally nonaggressive.
when the vet stapled his scrotum
(after big pulled out his neutering stitches)
he licked the man in the face.

but if he thinks a member of his pack is threatened...
big has got their back.

in one sense it is reassuring.
big could & would provide significant protection in a pinch.

on the other hand,
big will be staying on his leash,
unless i decide we really need that much protection.

laz

76

april 21, 2011
coach big

i've been pushing hard to get ready for the jim.
here in the home stretch,
i've finally made it up to 50-60 miles a week.
that isn't really much,
but, unable to run or even walk fast with my crippled leg,
i feel pretty good about it.

well, maybe "good" isn't exactly the right word.
spending 4 hours a day on the road can become a grind.
my bad leg hurts all the time,
but that is easy enough to get used to.
it is when everything else gets sore that it starts to bug me.
and it isn't always easy to keep going out
when you are tired and want a day off.

i don't put any days off in my schedule.
i just take off when it is raining
(can't afford to get my shoes wet,
they take forever to dry & it damages them)
thanks to weather radar,
(god bless weather radar)
i have been able to skip around the rainy days
starting my walks with rain on the way
and finishing before it arrives.
or waiting and going out as soon as the last of it passes.

but i have begun counting down the days until the last week,
when i can finally do my taper.
i've been praying for rain so i could get a day off.

maybe if i had me one of those "affirmations"
it would get easier to head out.
after all, i know if i want this, i will have to earn it.
but really, i get more motivation just from enjoying the
beautiful, quiet places i get to walk.
watching spring arrive.
watching the sunrise come earlier & sunset later each day.

77

no matter how tired & sore i get,
every day is great.

but that doesn't make it any easier to get my tired butt out of bed
or to hurry out after work,
when what i'd really like to do is sleep late in the morning,
or eat and kick back to watch some tv after work.
for that motivation i have to count on my coaches.

i have the best coaches in the business.
coach big and coach little.
coach little has her own style.
she approaches every workout with fire & enthusiasm.
you can't help but enjoy the day, with little along.
but she has four times as many good legs as i do.

big is the taskmaster...
and i can't complain about my problems,
when he is limping along on his own bad leg.
nobody shot me.

if i am late,
big has that PDA hidden in his bigloo
and he starts telling the world it is time to go.
if i think about cutting it short one day,
big just stops and looks at me.
then he looks on down the way we are supposed to go.
then he looks back at me again,
and you can read his thoughts,
"this isn't where we turn around...
if you really want it, you got to earn it."
"c'mon big. just this once? i am wore out."
"do you want to train to finish the race,
or practice making excuses for the dnf?"

big usually gets his way. how can you argue with someone who
only speaks with their eyes?

today looked like i was finally going to get a day off.
huge thunderstorms rolled in last night
(monster hailstorm about 0230 this morning)

at 0400 it was raining cats & dogs.
even big didn't complain when i just fed him breakfast
with no walk.

all day it was cold and dreary.
and more rain was coming tonight.
i was making all kinds of plans
they all revolved around warm dry clothes and a recliner.

if it weren't for coach big,
wednesday the 20th would have been a big zero.
when i fed him tonight, he ate part of his food.
then he came & "sat" in front of me.
none of his usual begging for petting
he just "sat"
and when he looked up,
those expressive yellow eyes said,
"where is my leash?"
"not tonight big, it's going to rain."
"it isn't raining now."

the look in his eyes was so forlorn.
and when i started for the house
the most piteous whimpers followed me.
i looked over my shoulder.
big always heads for the bigloo after supper,
without a complaint.
tonight his whimpers said;
"cut out my heart and stomp on it.
or skip our workout.
same difference."

instead of going in and taking off my muddy boots
i opened the back door & hollered at amy,
"will you bring me big's leash?"

if you work out for coach big,
you can't leave out coach little.
so when big & i got back,
little & i headed out.
as we walked, i started to hear thunder in the distance.

i told little, "if it starts raining, we are turning back."
and i started to wonder how wet i was going to get.

by the turnaround, the thunder was rumbling,
and an occasional flash of lightning could be seen.
i was humping along as fast as i could go.
the house, the thunder, the lightning, and my breaking point
were all converging.
all i could think was,
"this isn't one of those rains that starts slow & builds.
this one is going to hit like a tidal wave."

i was expecting a deluge every step up the last hill
pushing myself to the limit to beat it.
i didn't relax until i hit the back steps.
as i did, a huge flash of lightning exploded directly overhead.
a minute later the rains followed.

one more stone in the wall.
one more workout in the bank.
and i owe it all to coach big.
he must have a more advanced weather radar in his bigloo than
the one on tv.

i don't guess i need one of those affirmations after all.
not as long as i got coach big.

one thing worries me, tho.
i have a feeling coach big doesn't put much stock in "tapering."

laz

april 25, 2011
big easter-the depletion run

easter sunday was set aside for my depletion "run" for the jim, being a little less than 2 weeks before the race.

my plan was simple.
push myself hard and wear myself down.
after 3 weeks of "intense" training it would then be time to "listen to my body."
if i recover quickly, i will keep putting in good mileage, and do another depletion run next week. if i don't recover quickly, i will back off some and not do another depletion run.
the idea is to hit race day with the maximum combined effect of conditioning and being rested.
experience gives me a pretty good feel for where that will fall.

since i can't run, the mileage wasn't going to be great. and since i have lots of stuff to get done, not all my depletion "run" would be running. some of it was going to be chores.
to maximize the effect of my workout, i was not going to eat at all that day, except some chocolate at lunch.

coaches big & little started my day with 7 miles on the road. combined with the dog-swap in the middle, this took about 3 hours. i took no fluids along and had a single can of dr pop afterwards.

then i entered the brush-cutting segment of my run.
this lasted until lunch, then i had another dr pop & ate a little chocolate.

the afternoon was set aside for the "fun" part of my day:
hoeing the garden.
i put little in her pen, since she likes to help with everything, and she is truly little help with garden work.
as i got near the end, i was talking to little, & reached the point where i could see big's part of the yard.
i said, "well, little, i am almost done, even without the help of little and... big?"

big was lying on his side in the middle of his big yard, with his legs sticking straight out in the air, and his neck extended with his head flat on the ground.
i told little that, "i think your brother, big, is playing dead."
big didn't move a muscle."big? BIG?!"
still no response.

something was wrong. i could go to the innermost room in the house, cover my face with a pillow, and whisper "big", and he would start barking & jumping around outside.
i asked little, "what in the world has happened to big?"
and started over to check on him.
big just lay there, lifeless. "i don't think he's breathing, little."
just as i got to my "dead" dog, he leaped to his feet,
with that big silly grin on his face.
that dog just ain't right.
dogs don't play practical jokes, right?

hoeing complete, i decided it was time for a cold drink.
that really hit the spot and i decided, tired or not, i was up for a few more miles.

big and i went first.
this would be big's day to really shine.
buddy saw us coming down the road, and came running out.
buddy is a jerk.
ok, buddy is actually a nice dog,
but he doesn't listen.
he comes out and runs around us, tormenting big,
and the walk always turns into an ordeal.
buddy is the kind of dog who, when he knows he isn't wanted,
stays just out of kicking range.
(not that i would kick him with big along,
big might decide to help)
i was not happy to see buddy.
i was way too tired to have to wrestle big down the road.

well, big did pull out front to meet buddy.
big thinks it is his job to vet any other dog before they get to me.
but after that, he was big focused.
eyes ahead, steady pace.

buddy could run in circles & carry on all he wanted.
big was on duty. he treated our walk like he was guarding the
tomb of the unknown soldier.

god bless big.

laz

april 28, 2011
weather disaster

very active weather morning.
saw several pictures of funnel clouds within a couple of miles of
the house, and had two "radar detected" tornados go right over
us, but fortunately suffered nothing like the damage in alabama.

woke up to heavy rain and wind & knew i wouldn't be walking,
so i started to fix big some breakfast.
it dawned on me i should turn on the tv
and see what the situation was.
the tv came on to a tornado warning, and a radar picture with
their "tornado" symbol, right on top of my house!
i had just enough time to think, "i need to go get big!"
when all hell broke loose.
sideways rain, trees whipping around.
i went & looked out the window to check on big, and he was
barely visible thru the maelstrom...
just standing there like a statue, right in the middle of it all.
he didn't look real happy, but there wasn't anything to be done
about it at that moment.

it was over in just a couple of minutes and i went out to one
drenched dog.
his topless bigloo was filled with water
(maybe he wasn't so clever to dismantle it).
i dried him as best i could, and dumped the bigloo and dried it,
fed him, and had to go to work.
i was late getting there.
got turned back twice by roads with trees down,
and once for a flooded bridge.
the road that i finally got thru on had three trees across it, but
they had already been moved to the side.

storms continued all day at work, we even had to go to the
basement once for a tornado warning.

but the biggest unease of the day was driving home. i had to
detour around a couple of flooded roads, and was approaching

the house from the north, when the radio announced another
tornado warning in south rutherford county.
i didn't have to wonder where it was, i could see it.
there was not time to do anything but pull over, about a quarter
mile from the house, before it went right over me in my car.
that was not cool.

when i got to the house, there stood poor big.
he had been thru his second tornado of the day,
and was again soaked to the skin,
his bigloo topless and filled with water.

he looked truly miserable. i turned the bigloo upside down to
drain thoroughly, and took him to the porch and stayed out there
with him until i got him completely dry and warm.
when he saw the leash, naturally he wanted to go walking and
acted disappointed when i took him up on the porch instead.
i am not near as dedicated as big.

by the time he was good and dry, the rain had ended, so i went
and dried out the bigloo and filled it with a large pile of dry
straw. big looked really happy, and burrowed in until he was
nearly invisible and went to sleep.

i don't know the stories behind his missing tooth, or the huge
scar on his throat.
but, since i have known him he has been dumped, shot,
abandoned, and now he has been thru two tornados in one day.
he is going to have quite an autobiography to write.

laz

may 07, 2011
the big run

the day of the strolling jim finally came.
it was such a shame that big could not be there,
but i could not both do the race, and focus on making certain that
big was alright.
pit bulls are not generally welcome in crowds.

in one sense, big was there.
without his insistence on getting in our miles, regardless of the
conditions, without the example of his own refusal to concede to
his injured leg, i probably would not have succeeded.

14 months after the vascular surgeon told me that people with
legs like mine, "talk about walking in terms of steps, not miles"
i walked the 41.2 miles of the strolling jim in eighteen and a half
hours.

forget that i once could run the same event in six and a half
hours.

i crossed the finish line feeling like a champion.

i had not just rescued the big. we had rescued each other.

laz

may 12, 2011
big news

for all of big's friends out there,
there was some not surprising news this morning.

tony will not be returning to reclaim big.
part of me is glad.
i have enjoyed working with big the last few months.
part of me is sad.
big's life is an unending series of abandonments.
all he has ever wanted is to be someone's loyal friend,
but he has seen several "owners" walk away,
never to return.

they were going to advertise big on craigslist,
but i sent word to abandon that effort.
i cannot give big to just some person who shows up.
big thinks he belongs to me.
besides, it seems like most people who want pit bulls
actually have no business with one.

i have to get past the hurdle of his supposed "temporary" status.
i can't deny his training has gone well.
he is ready to graduate.
he approaches his coaching duties with solemn seriousness,
focused on doing his job.
he doesn't even take off after squirrels & rabbits
(as much as he'd like to)
altho yesterday, when a rabbit came from right under his feet
he jumped about 3 feet straight up in the air...
twice.
then he looked up at me & grinned proudly.

he did a good job with company during jim weekend,
jumping on no one,
greeting people with dignity.
but making himself available for petting
(just in case someone needed to pet a big)

i think it is time to ask permission to construct a big-proof home
(i am thinking brick or stone *might* be strong enough)

wish me luck.

laz

part 4: routines

the big family

hello. my name is big.
i am a very busy dog.
i have lots of important work to do with my master.
and i have a family to protect.

master has a good family
and i am an important member.
there are the other dogs,
a white dog named little
and a black dog named sophie.
sophie is afraid of me, and will not play.
little is not afraid of anything, and she loves to play.

there are the girl and the lady master.
the girl is my special charge.
she is very good to me.
i go with her to run.
i love to run, but i am there to protect her.
the lady master is different.
she never pets me or speaks to me,
but i know she is very important to the master.
i can tell these things.

when no one else is there at mealtime,
the lady master feeds me.
i know that she likes me.
i can tell these things.
but she never pets me or speaks to me.

the master does not need protecting.
he is never afraid of anything.
i feel very safe with master.
but when he is not there it is my job to protect the family.

i am very happy here with my family.
this is where i belong.

big dog

may 20, 2011
big fears

i saw them before big did; a little clump of about 8 bicyclists
sweeping around a curve, about a half mile away.
i immediately took us to the other side of the road, and
commanded big, "SIT...STAY"

big obediently sat & looked up at me, awaiting his release, so we
could continue the walk. then he heard the whir of the
approaching bikes, and his eyes got wide.
he turned his head to watch them approach
conflicting urges to obey his commands and to flee in terror were
obvious, so i reached down to stroke his head and calm him.

as they got to us, one of the cyclists called out, "thanks!"
i suppose there is no harm done in them thinking i was worried
about big scaring them.
as the mini-peleton passed, big finally broke from his sitting
position and took a step towards the ditch in preparation to flee.
but, by then the bikes were past us, disappearing up the road the
way we had come.

big is terrified of bicycles. there is a lot in his past that i don't
know about, but i think we have all heard the stories about
bicyclists' unprovoked attacks on innocent pit bulls.
whether he is just responding to their strangeness, or he has
some unfortunate incident in his secret past, big is terrified of
bicycles.

after the first unexpected encounter, when a fleeing big nearly
dragged me into a cow pasture
(i had expected him to pay them little attention,
if i paid them little attention)
we have been working on his fear.
distracting him with orders to "SIT" and "STAY," he is getting
close to being able to stay calm while they pass.
one day, i hope we can just walk on as they go by.
but that day hasn't come yet.
he will need to get a lot more used to them than he is now.

we don't see them that frequently, but our quiet little road
seems to be on a lot of bikers list of riding routes.
over time, we probably see more total bicycles than cars, because
we never see one bike. when they come, they come in packs.
one day more than 30 went by us in about 5 minutes.

anyway, when we continued, the spell of our walk was broken.
big kept looking over his shoulder, as if they might come back
and hurrying ahead of me,
wanting to put as much distance between him and those hell
machines as possible.
most of the time, he seems to understand,
"big, the more you pull, the slower we go. i have to lean back &
pull against you, to keep from being pulled onto my face."
today, he didn't care.
so we turned around early, and headed for the house.

now, we were going right towards where the bicycles had
disappeared.
this was not big's idea of a good plan
and he started hanging back.
then he got behind me, and was peeking around my legs
watching for the horsemen of the apocalypse to return.

how could i keep from laughing.
the big dog.
100 pounds of muscle, bone, & sinew,
with a head the size of a bowling ball.
i imagine every cyclist on earth would have their blood run cold
if they saw big waiting in the road.
and there he was looking around my legs,
like a child peeking around mama's skirt.

it is a good thing i could see the humor.
because he kept bumping into my legs.
big is wide and squat.
it would take a car to knock him off his feet.
i am not that stable.
but nothing was going to get him any further from me than
absolutely necessary.

big isn't afraid of a whole lot.
but he has had one other noticable fear.
children.

i don't recall there being any child issues during his first tenure,
but after tony abandoned him, he was at a place where he was
chained in the yard all day and the neighborhood children would
gather and throw rocks at him.
that had to be a miserable time for big.
for a dog defined by his love of people,
the pain of being stoned while trapped on a chain is emotional as
well as physical.
he came back to me very leery of children.

thanks to the girls next door, laura kate and anna grace,
the child issue is fading.
around here, when a neighbor passes us walking,
they stop to talk.
big will just sit patiently & wait for us to continue our walk.
sometimes it is ben or susan,
with their two sweet little girls along.
after a few of those visits,
big doesn't even scare the mother any more.

so i asked the girls if they wanted to pet big,
telling them he might be a little afraid of them.
the plan was, each time they stopped,
they would just call to big to come over to them.
this is always better than approaching a dog that is afraid of you.
if he didn't go to them, we would just continue on our way.
the first few times, he sort of shied away.
but the last time he carefully eased over within reach & stood
there happily while laura kate patted him on his massive head.

little by little, big is conquering his fears.
i am glad...
i owe him something for all the good coaching i am getting.

laz

may 27, 2011
big lightshow

maybe he hears my eyes open.

i don't know how he does it,
but coach big knows when i wake up.
i'll be sitting there on the side of my bed,
with my lazy self arguing that this is the perfect day to not go out
& walk, while my (much weaker) industrious self is trying to
think of a reason to go,
when i will start to hear coach big's call to arms.
to my human ears, his barks sound like faint squeaks...
i mean, he is outside, at the far end of the house.

but he knows i am awake before my feet touch the floor.
he must hear my eyes open.

and i think he can read my mind, as well.
because his call to arms is a much stronger argument to get up
and go than anything i can think of.
and big *never* thinks it is a good day to take off.

i am never sorry that i answered his call.
coach big knows the best part of the day is always just ahead.

it is pitch black when i go out the door.
big greets me with his joyous, "wooo---wooo---wooo."
"i hear you, big. see what i have?"
i hold up the blue leash he loves more than anything he owns.
i don't know if big can see, but he knows what i have.
he always knows.
i can't see anything but blackness as i go over to get my training
partner.
but i know where he is.
leaping into the air, and turning his crazy flips.
i can hear his feet hitting the ground.
i can hear him puffing and panting like a steam engine.
when i know i am getting close, i tell him,
"DOWN, stay DOWN big fella. don't you jump on me."

and then i can hear him skittering across the ground.
i laugh at the unseen sight, because i have seen it so many times.
he will be sitting alright, his whole body vibrating with
excitement, till he literally skitters across the ground
like one of those old-timey electric football figures.

darkness doesn't matter.
i know where to find big.
as soon as i am in reach, he will be sitting directly in front of me
with his head leaned against my legs.
knowing he will have his cable stretched so tight that i can't get it
off,
i move around him, and take a step further into his space.
frantically he scoots around until he is back in front of me.

once i clip on his leash, and drop his cable on the ground,
big transforms into a dog under total control.
he stands up and waits, statue-like, for me to get started.

by the time we reach the bottom of the hill,
the pre-dawn light is just enough to make out the land around
me.
i come around the corner, and the sight of the winston's place
takes my breath away.
i can see about a hundred acres of pasture,
and it is twinkling with millions of fireflies.

when i was a boy, the fireflies were out like this every night.
their decline over the past 30 years has stolen some of the magic
from the night.
these days, all i usually see are isolated flashes, here and there.

but this morning is totally magical.
countless fireflies,
as many as the stars in the sky,
are twinkling as far as the eye can see.

and they are everywhere this morning.
i stop several times to just drink in the vision.
ben and susan's farm is a 200 acre vista of flickering flashes,
a magnificent light show for big & i, that no one else will see.

100

i tell big about how, when i was a boy,
it was like this every night in the summer.
and how i would run around barefooted in the soft grass,
collecting dozens of fireflies in a mayonnaise jar
to set them on my dresser
& lie in bed & watch them flash until i drifted off to sleep.
big just looks out at the fields & listens with his usual solemnity.

by the time we make our turn & start back
the morning is dawning & the fireflies are heading back to their
hiding places.
but the show is safely stored in my memory.
i have but to close my eyes, and i can see it again.

i know that big and i got in our miles that morning.
i remember all the places we went, and how they looked.
but it was as if we were transported there without effort.
the magic of that special morning carried us.

we have a goal, big and i.
the end is supposed to be realized on bloody 11w,
when i reach bristol in less than 72 hours.
but every step along the way reveals its own treasures,
every day we go out has something special
something in that moment, that can never be duplicated
but can be relived forever.
this day it was the fireflies.

before that, it was the morning displays by the tom turkeys;
strutting, resplendent in their colorful mating finery
on their impromptu dance floors in the pasture
each trying to show the other up,
while the hens gathered around,
gossiping and watching their favorites out of the corner of their
eyes
pretending indifference.

before we know it, it will be the squadrons of young turkeys
following their mothers around the same pastures.

an endless string of memories are out there.

bobcats hunting rabbits in the brush,
the rise & fall of the 13 year cicadas,
the deer, the hawks, the owls,
the cycles and rhythms of the life around us.

big is a wise coach.
he knows the best part of the day is always just ahead,
the best part of the year is just starting,
and the best day of our lives is today.

and i swear, when i wake up he can hear my eyes open.

laz

june 01, 2011
big tricks

a number of people had written,
concerned about poor big living on a cable.
i will be the first to admit that i never saw myself having a dog on
a cable in the yard.
i always thought that was a cruel way to treat a dog.

big had different ideas.
while big doesn't seem to mind his cable,
he does not like being enclosed.
AT ALL!

crates, pens, fences, locked doors;
all are anathema to the big.
when he first arrived with his bullet wound,
he was supposed to be crated for a week or two while he healed.
for a couple of days this worked well.
big was too injured to do anything but lay there,
except being brought out to feed or use the bathroom.
after he got a little strength back, he demonstrated that he was
the uncrateable dog.
big had a variety of tricks to defeat nearly any latch created by
man...
the nose push, until the latch popped. "stretching" the crate, to
change the angle so the nose push worked,
finding a seam that he could get his nose into,
and then following his nose thru
big can get thru any space in which his nose will fit.
not that big can compress to fit a hole the size of his nose.
it is the hole which must adapt and become the size of a big.
and if those failed, he simply demolished the crate.

next he defeated pens & fences.
he can burrow like a mole.
confront him with a rock floor, he can leap a 4 foot fence.
thwart him with a 6 foot fence, he can bite thru chain link.
big is the consumate escape artist.

during his time as an indoor dog,
a rule was soon implemented that big never be placed behind a
closed door.
big is able to open doors.
even if it means taking them off their hinges.
he also dislikes closed windows.
big likes to feel free,
and so any curtains or shades, well they have to come down.
don't want to take your curtains down?
no problem, big will take care of that for you...
carefully, so as not to damage the curtains.

so big is on a cable.
but he isn't just stuck out in the middle of the yard.
big's home is in the edge of the woods.
he has lots of shade,
and he enjoys just laying there looking out into the woods.

of course, this means big has a number of trees in his space.
for every dog i ever owned,
that would be an insurmountable obstacle.
i had come to believe that dogs simply cannot grasp the concept
of wrapping their chain around a tree.
but big can untangle himself with ease.
when big wraps his cable around a tree,
he stops, studies the situation, then slowly & deliberately walks
back around the tree to get free.

big gets lots of company, and frequent off cable time
(so he can train me for my races).
as case pointed out the first time he visited,
big rushes out to greet visitors,
but stops 6 inches short of the end of his cable.
there he jumps around and goes nuts.
he only reaches the end of his cable when he is doing flips.
when he sees me bringing his blue leash, he goes nuts.
he calls out to me, "wooo---wooo---wooo"
while stomping his front feet in a stacatto drumbeat:
right-left-right-left-right-left
then he leaps up like a ballerina, pirouetting in the air,
and finally he will do his flips;

104

leaping to the end of the cable and, when it stops his head,
flipping his body over and turning in the air to land on his feet.
he seems very proud of his flips.
when he first started them he didn't always land on his feet, but
now he is quite proficient.
i hardly feel worthy of such a performance.
(i think it is for the blue leash, anyway)

the onset of tennessee summer has brought big new problems to
solve.
big is not a hot weather dog, and really was having a hard time of
it.
to seek relief, he would go to his water bowl, take one big paw,
and flip water on himself.
it didn't take long before the water was all gone,
and all that was in the bottom of the bowl was a little mud.
we wondered how he was drinking so much, even in the heat.
then he started just dumping the bowl over, and laying in the
cool mud.

either technique meant he was soon barking his "help me" bark.
he had no water to drink.

so we bought big his own above ground pool.
amy set it up for him,
and when she brought out the first gallon of water
(filling it to a depth of about a millimeter)
big hopped right in and stood there grinning.

we have continued to fill it a gallon at a time...
if we were rich, we'd own a longer hose.
if we were big, we'd figure out a better way!
and big is loving it.
standing in the water,
or splashing it all over himself,
with a look of joy on his ugly face.

big is just full of tricks.
my favorite; amy already told you about.
amy was lying out on the front porch, sunbathing.
i was looking out the window at big.

big walked down to the end of his area where he could see the
front porch.
he looked at amy for a minute or so,
then he walked very deliberately over to a tree
and wrapped his cable around it...
stepping carefully over the cable as he completed the loop.
then he walked toward amy until the cable was taut,
and began barking his "help me" bark.

he has this trick down to an art form.
if amy comes to "save him" he is overwhelmingly grateful.
but, if she doesn't notice him,
he will soon give up, unwrap his cable,
and go back to lie in the shade.
that dog makes me nervous.
dogs don't have frontal lobes, right?

so this episode is just further evidence that my dog is a genius.
my daughter, however,
is slathering herself with spf 100 sunscreen...
and then going out and lying in the sun.
which seems to me like driving with the parking brake on.

maybe i can get big to have a talk with her.

laz

june 07, 2011
big-the killer instinct comes out

Living in the edge of the woods,
big dog has to deal with the usual nemeses of all outdoorsmen:
arthropods.
(insects and arachnids to be more specific)
i havent been able to tell if he ever gets chiggers,
but he does pick up a few ticks.

when i find a tick, i just tell him to "hold still"...
a command he seems to understand...
while i pull them off.
then i put them on a flat rock in his space
(the killing rock)
and squish them with a smaller rock.
big then has to carefully inspect what i "got off him."

more troublesome are the occasional biting insects.
being at the top of a hill, he doesn't face too many of those,
but there are always some.
the other day i came out to find big standing as if at attention
head stiffly erect, with his eyes crossed
(a crosseyed pit bull actually looks pretty intimidating)
when i got closer, i could see a mosquito hovering right above
the tip of his nose.
big was watching the mosquito!
"hold still" i told him,
and then clapped my hands together about a half inch from his
nose.
big didn't flinch, but he insisted on seeing the mosquito corpse...
and then grinned his approval.

sometimes we will come home from a walk,
and a deerfly will show up to feast on big (or me)
again, a simple "hold still" and big is a statue.
i try to squash the fly with a clap on takeoff,
but sometimes i have to slap them on big.
he never flinches, even when i smack one on his head.
he just insists on seeing the corpse.

what i worried about was what he did when i wasn't around.
i hated to think of him just getting eaten alive,
with no way to respond.

i worry no longer.

i had just finished taking care of big
and was getting ready to carry his food bowl and water jugs back
to the house
when a sudden movement caught my eye.
big was snapping at a biting fly buzzing around his head.
i started to tell him to "hold still" and "i will handle it"
but i decided to see how he dealt with his tormentor.
big didn't look like he was just going to accept getting bit.

he ran the fly off from trying to land on his head,
but we all know biting flies never give up until they are dead.
big knows it, too.
he jumped to his feet, and was whipping his head around from
side to side,
so he could see his butt.
when the fly tried to land there, he snapped at it again.
a couple more futile snaps, and big headed for his pool.
he got right in the middle
and stood there,
whipping his head around to watch his back end.
when the fly came back for more,
he snapped at it a couple more times,
then he either knocked it into the water, or it flew into the water.

no matter how it happened, big was ready.
in the twinkling of an eye, he took his paw and pushed the fly
underwater.
he watched the surface intently, and when the fly surfaced, he
pushed it under again.

by the time he had pushed it underwater a few times,
the fly stopped struggling.
big then gently picked up the corpse with his front teeth,
carried it over to a clear spot on the other side of his bigloo,
laid it on the ground and inspected it carefully.

108

so big dog really is a killer at heart.
and now i have something new to worry about.
he isn't just a threat to maul someone.
he could just as easily push them into his pool,
and hold their head underwater until they drown.

i am pretty sure this isn't really a dog.
naresh would probably tell me that he is a good person
who died and came back as a higher being.

laz

june 13, 2011
jumping rope with big

june is the time stu & i make our annual pilgrimage to paducah
(the land where being in the river & next to the river is a matter
of a one or two percents of humidity)
to run in the kentucky durby
(some call it the run under the stars).
the durby is a really neat event, 10 hours from 2000 hours
saturday evening until 0600 on sunday morning, held on a 1/2
mile horse track.

stu came up friday night & saturday morning i slept in
(until 0700!)
so that i would be well rested for an all-night effort.

i had just finished feeding big, refilling his pool, etc.
and was just sitting there apologizing for not taking our morning
walk and telling him i was going to be gone until tomorrow,
when stu came out.

little was in the pen,
because when she and big are playing, nobody wants to be
within reach of big's cable.
little's favorite game is to race thru big's area,
with big tearing around in pursuit.
big's cable operates like a daisy cutter,
leveling anything inside its radius.

i heard stu ask, "is it all right if i let little out?"
and i started to answer, "sure; just..."
the rest of my answer was supposed to be, "let me get clear first."
instead of finishing my answer, i saw little fly past me at full
speed & said, "crap!"
big took off in hot pursuit, and i jumped to my feet as fast as my
old bones would move...

just in time for big's cable to wrap around my left ankle & chop
me down like a tree.

i hit the ground, slipped my foot out of the cable, and leapt to my
feet again just as little whizzed back past me.
amy can tell you; when you know it is coming,
avoiding big's cable is like a high stakes game of jump-rope.

my jump came just a moment too late,
and the cable clipped the toe of my right foot as it hummed past
under me.
i went down on my face, again.
this time, with no cable wrapped around my leg, i bounced back
up like a rubber ball & scrambled out of reach before little could
come back thru.
stumbling, i reached out and grabbed a tree to catch my balance.
a locust tree.
the long thorns punctured my palm in 4 places,
adding a bloody palm to the cable-burn around my leg.
stu laughed heartily...
even tho it was an accident he let little out, with me still on the
firing line.
at least i think it was an accident.

laz

june 22, 2011
training with mr big-wild roses and apparitions

one of the parts of my training that i enjoy is watching the parade
of wildflowers go past.
nature seems to have conspired to provide the pollinators with a
never ending buffet
as first one type of flower, and then another, bursts into bloom.
each separate species has its own day in the sun.
some of them i know by name. most, only by their appearance.
the tennessee wild rose show has just ended.
(further north & east, they are known as the virginia wild rose!)

they are one of my favorites,
altho they are not even native plants.
but rather are long-ago imports from europe or asia,
which have now naturalized themselves into the american
woodlands.

the wild rose grows in big clumped tangles of vines,
along fencerows, in the edge of the woods, or on streambanks.
they bloom along the entirety of the vines forming starbursts of
white or pink,
like frozen firework displays.

they have now been replaced as the dominant blossoms
by a white flower that grows in big bunches atop weed-like
stalks.

big was particularly insistent this morning,
as he issued his "time to get to work" call.
it rained all day yesterday,
and he spent most of the day sitting on the surviving base of the
demolished bigloo, keeping dry.

and with a cool breeze blowing this morning,
in place of the previous week's suffocating muggy heat,
big was raring to go.
once we got on the road, he required frequent reminders
that this was not a laz-towing event.

big has his own agenda as we walk.
he runs his nose a mile a minute,
keeping tabs on what wild animals crossed his road during the
night, and he has a radar for spotting deer, turkey, rabbits,
or any other animal that we really ought to chase...
if i weren't such a spoilsport.
if the coyotes have been around, big gets all worked up.
all in all, while i pride myself on all the wildlife i spot,
i doubt i detect 10% of the animals big does.

big, like all dogs, has to leave a message at all his favorite sign
posts.
he doesn't have little's desire to spend a lot of time reading the
messages left by other dogs.
he just washes them all away with his water cannon,
and leaves his one big message:
"THIS IS BIG'S ROAD!"

he also maintains a remarkable inventory of everything that is in
his road.
if there is a new stick that fell from a tree,
or a dirt clod that fell off a tractor,
we have to swerve over to give it a quick sniff and identify it.
cigarette packs and beer cans get the same treatment.
but only once.
after big has identified the object in his road,
he has no further interest in it.

one day there was a plastic hood off a utility light in the road.
it was so dark that i wasn't certain what it was,
so i didn't let big go check it out for a couple of days,
until the sun came up early enough & i could see what it was.

big's anxiety about the URO (unidentified road object)
got more intense every day,
until the day i let him check it out
he practically ran over to it.
one sniff & he looked up at me with disdain;
"crimonettles, it's just a piece of plastic!"

while big mostly looks at the close range"
(altho his scent-view covers both space and time)
i like to look off in the fields and up in the sky a lot.
there is a point of convergence, however,
between my and big's fields of observation.
we both look at all the things along the roadside.

this morning we went out to the turnaround uneventfully,
but about halfway back i could sense big tensing up.
he started dropping back,
until he was in his uncertain position...
behind me, peering around my legs.

following his gaze,
i took a start myself.
about a hundred yards ahead
and just on the other side of the ditch
a white figure stood in the halflight
with its arms outstretched like a scarecrow.

as we approached the apparition
big drew closer and closer behind me
until he was practically stepping on my heels.
his faith in me is touching
but, realistically, we are not going to meet anyone or anything
that wouldn't prefer fighting me to facing big.
(i could not, for example, take a man's entire head in my mouth &
crush it like a grape)

by the time we got within 20 yards,
big was strongly suggesting we stop and go the other way,
or at the very least cross the road.
my own confidence was bolstered by the fact the apparition had
not moved.
i was fairly certain it was inanimate.
it was only a matter of getting close enough to see what it was.

as we closed the last few steps,
the ghostly figure separated into a patch of the new white
flowers,
with the gleaming white bunches of blossoms

aligning themselves into a perfect scarecrow shape when seen
straight on from a distance,
altho the arms & torso were actually in clumps spread out along
10 to 20 feet, and the head was still further up the road.

big relaxed and looked up at me.
in the dim light i was pretty sure i detected a sheepish grin.
altho he cast several cautious glances at the flowers as we
walked by as if they might magically recombine into some sort of
woodland demon.
after we had passed, i looked back.
sure enough, from this side there was nothing but an ordinary
patch of wildflowers.
later on, in better light, the figure was gone from either direction
as distance perspective returned with full visibility.
like so many things we see on our daily "runs"
it was only there for that one moment in time.

the remainder of the walk passed without incident
and by the time we reached the house we were in full light.
i brought big his breakfast
and afterward we took a break & talked about "things"
before big finally walked over to his current favorite lounging
spot and lay down.
then he looked at me, as if to say,
"you can go on to work now. i will see you this afternoon..."
"don't be late!"

laz

june 25, 2011
big's happy day

into every runner's life a little downtime must fall.
in between the jim, and gearing up for my 100 mile attempt at
bloody 11w
i've only been going out once a day.
splitting time between big & little, that means big is only getting
about an hour a day of walking.
and the poor guy hasn't gotten to run at all since he last slipped
his leash...
that was months ago.

altho he can still jump as high as my head,
and do flips,
big has gotten visibly flabby.

not fat, but the muscle tone has markedly declined.
there isn't much i can do about it.
i cannot run, and if i keep going at 50-60 miles a week without
some downtime
(an effort equal to 120-140 miles a week back when i was young
and healthy)
i will just break down.

this morning, big & i were a little late getting started
and amy was already out on the road.
i was talking with big, apologizing that i couldn't give him a
better workout,
as we came around the winston corner and saw amy walking
toward us.
an idea that had been tickling the back of my brain came to the
front.

when we finally met, i asked amy if she might want to try out big
running.
he'd gotten most of his bad habits out of the way,
and i thought he was about ready to run with someone who
couldn't actually physically control him.

amy was game. she is very fond of big.
i handed her the leash.
amy broke into a run, and big fell in beside her like a pro.
what a beautiful sight he is when he runs.
the picture of power and grace.

he glanced over his shoulder a time or two,
to make sure i was there
but he was loving every step of the way.
after a few hundred yards,
they turned and ran back to me.
when they got there
big's eyes gleamed with pure joy

we talked and walked the rest of the way.
sophie has a bad hip, and more than a couple of miles a day
makes her limp.
amy is planning her first 50 mile
(and looking for recommendations, by the way, for a low-cost
50)
and can use all the miles she can get.
i think it is a match made in heaven...
as amy opined, she would feel pretty safe running with big.
(no one will come by and think, "look, a girl with a friendly
puppy, lets give them trouble.")
and big needs the work.
the exercise will be good for him, and he feels important when he
has an athlete to train.

they ran again before we finished the morning walk,
going another few hundred yards and then waiting for me.
big's grin was visible from 200 yards away
that dog has a face that just lights up when he is happy
and this morning he was as happy as any dog can be.

the rest of the way home, big walked next to amy.
sure, i had the leash again,
but he had to be ready, in case amy needed to run some more.

so it looks like amy will be splitting time.
running sophie's couple of miles,

then big the rest of whatever she is doing.
she's gonna find out that coach big is a demanding trainer.
he doesn't think much of days off
and he isn't all that high on tapering, either.

once he finds out she is going to regularly take him running,
amy will find out about dedication to training.
big can hear my eyes open at the far end of the house.
amy is in the room nearest the big.
at least until amy moves, things look good for that lucky dog.
this was truly big's happy day.

laz

july 05, 2011
big players and rabbit gangs

it is easy to forget how big looks to strangers.
most of the people who come by the house know of big,
even if they haven't met him yet.
big, for his part, seems to love everybody,
and revels in his role as ambassador of goodwill.
as case noted one day, "big seems to love all people,
even tho everything we know about his history
ought to have made him hate people."

last week we hosted a group of former nba & wnba players
who were holding a basketball camp at the local high school.
(luckily for us, not everyone thought to put a dorm in their
house)
seeing that they all seemed to like little & sophie
i suggested a trip to the backyard to meet big.

only one guy went with me, and he wouldn't get anywhere close
to big.
he just wanted to know if big was, "only tied up with a rope, or
do you have him on a chain?"
for the rest of the week everyone was happy enough to look at
big thru the window.
i think they only wanted to be sure he was still secured,
before going to their cars.

our guests being athletes,
athletes committed to running a maximum of 94 feet at a time,
they were astonished at amy's running.
having run 41 miles was an achievement almost beyond
comprehension.
(i think amy got a real charge out of that)
but what really amazed them was that amy ran with big...
"you run with HIM? he is TWICE your size!"

they simply underestimated big's desire to please.
this is a dog who,
after sitting & waiting patiently for permission to eat,

when given the release command will sniff his food,
then come over to be petted before eating.
it is as if he is saying, "thank you."
big does his walks & runs with intense concentration,
always striving to do his "important job" to perfection.

his greatest challenge comes from the rabbits.
i am pretty sure our short creek rabbits belong to a gang;
i call them the "short hares."
their favorite mischievous acts are darting in front of cars
to try and cause a wreck (or at least heart failure),
and tempting well behaved dogs to disobey the laws of the
leash...

altho it has yet to be proven they are not the ones knocking
down mailboxes up and down millersburg road.
if they had opposable thumbs,
i bet the whole neighborhood would be tagged.

these devilish rabbits will sit frozen in the center of the road,
until big & i nearly step on them
before hopping ahead a short ways & repeating the process.
other times they will hide in the weeds alongside the road
and then dart across in front of us,
almost under big's nose.

big tries to do right.
but you can see him tense when the rabbits are tantalizing him.
and sometimes he can't help but take that first step when one
dashes by right in front of him.
this isn't a major issue for me.
laz has more than ample counterweight to absorb a big jump.
amy, on the other hand,
while not half big's actual size, is no bigger than him
and not nearly as strong
(not to mention, she has no 4-wheel drive)
if big takes that "first step" with amy on the other end of the
leash, he nearly yanks her off her feet.

one day last week,
amy & big had just reached the end of the driveway

122

when big succumbed to temptation and took that first step.
amy, as is prescribed by house law,
promptly turned around and brought him back home.

big was disconsolate.
he lay forlornly about for the whole day.
when amy sat on the porch & read,
he didn't pretend to tangle his cable & call for help.
he didn't even come over & look hopeful for petting.

the next morning, when i came for his early walk
(for some reason amy doesn't get up at 0400)
big was ready.
he was determined to have the perfect walk.
he didn't pull the leash taut,
he didn't flinch when the gangsta rabbits teased him
he never even attempted to mark HIS road...
and altho amy doesn't stop for it,
we have our places i allow him to mark.

when we got home & hooked him back up,
he had a look of utter joy on his broad face.
his big, yellow-green eyes were glowing with pride,
and he was rocking back & forth,
shifting his weight between his front feet.
"woo, woo, woo" he said softly.
i understood what he meant.
"i'll tell amy how good you did, mr big.
that was your best walk ever."

big might make a 6-9, 280 pound man's blood run cold.
but amy has that puppy wrapped around her little finger.

laz

july 06, 2011
just put big in charge

it is like goundhog day out here in the woods.

we have our morning routine
and big believes it is his responsibility to keep us on track.

around 0400 i wake up.
(this morning it was 0409)
i can barely open my eyes when i hear big out back
telling me we have miles to log.
this is how our routine always begins.

get up, go to the bathroom
routine routine
put on my shorts & shoes
routine, routine
fill up big's food bowl
(he is like feeding a new holland hay baler)
grab his big blue leash
routine routine
little raises up her head as i pass her on the way out.
seeing the big blue leash, she yawns & lays back down for
another hour of sleep.
routine routine
set big's bowl on the porch & head out towards the bigloo
i can hear big in the darkness
jumping around and doing his flips
(someday i gotta get amy to take a picture of his flips)
"what is it big? is there something you want?"
routine routine
he vibrates with excitement 'til i get him hooked up
then he transforms instantly into mr discipline
and we are off
routine routine
we walk at a steady pace.
big marks his usual spots
the short hares are waiting to challenge his self control
just where they always wait.

i make note of how much later the sun is than yesterday
me & big talk about the weather
and whatever else comes up.
routine routine
about 5:15 we return to the bigloo.
i transfer big back to his cable
and go get his food & a gallon of water off the porch.
put big's food on the ground & tell him to wait.
while big sits & looks at his food
i dump his leftover drinking water into his aboveground pool
refill his drinking water & pour the rest of the gallon into his
pool.
then i release him to eat.
big goes over & sniffs at his food bowl

"same thing as yesterday, big guy,
maybe tomorrow we'll have some fat or something special."

big comes over and leans against me so i can pat his head.
"you're welcome, big fella."
big seems to be grateful for whatever i bring him.
then he goes back and eats.
while big eats, i just enjoy the view into the woods.
amy is supposed to come out with sophie about now,
so sophe can start her morning rituals.
"wonder where amy is this morning, big guy? she's a little late."
how can she break the routine?
after big is finished there is a little more petting,
then he goes over & lays down to rest up for his next workout.
it's a busy coach who has two athletes to train.
big loves to feel important.
"it's time for little's walk, mr big. i'll see you after a while."
back in the routine.

when little sees me pick up her leash,
she is up and ready to go.
just like big, she has her own routines to go thru,
altho we can vary the walk a bit more.
while we are gone, amy will run with the sophster,
& come back for big's turn.
i can judge our progress by where we see amy & big.

126

if i only catch a glimpse of them going around the winston corner
as little and i approach the driveway, we are late.
if we meet them in the driveway, we are early.
if we meet at the junction of driveway & road, we are both right
on time.

(one day i half expect her to say, "Phil? Hey, Phil? Phil! Phil
Connors? Phil Connors, I thought that was you!")
routine routine

this morning we don't see them at all.

when we get to the house, big starts barking his "help" bark.
i look around the corner of the house
and big is jumping up and down & barking at me.
"what is it big? did amy oversleep?"
routine broken!
(is it finally february 3?)

big quits barking as i head for the house.
he thinks i can fix anything wrong.
(and what can be more wrong than a broken routine?)

we go in and little 'sits' for her leash to come off
(handy tip for dog-runners, teach them to wait for a release
command when you remove the leash. that way you don't lose
an arm if you misfire unfastening it)
"little, go see if sophie is awake."
little heads around the corner for amy's room.

i am cheating here.
the first thing little does is always to go see where sophie is,
if sophe doesn't meet us at the door little is concerned.
(they are the "dog team" all day)

there is no ignoring a little sniffing under your door...
in just a minute amy & sophie come out yawning.
"where you been, sleepyhead?"
"i overslept."
"big is concerned."
"he didn't bark when it was time to go."

127

"you didn't open your eyes."
(ask amy, he really can hear your eyes open)

she pauses. "it is tough going from 4 miles a day to 6"
"you might need more sleep till you get used to it."
"do you know what it is like to get up every day at 5am?"
"yeah, it would be like sleeping in?"
(nothing like a smartaleck to start your day off right)

while i am feeding little, amy & sophie head out.
after i shave, shower, & get ready for work, i see sophie is back.
as i head for the car to go to work,
i detour to look at the bigloo.
it is vacant.
big's cable (tellingly) lies empty on the ground.
i smile to myself.
back in the routine!
all is well in big's world.
big never oversleeps,
he never seeks to vary the routine.
we ought to just put big in charge.

laz

part 5: contentment

big walks

hello. my name is big and i am a very busy dog.
i have a lot of important work to do.

my most important job is the one master calls "walk."
we have a very large territory to patrol.
master says it is "50 square miles."
i do not know how much that is,
but i know we walk for a long time every morning.

we walk a different way every day.
sometimes we walk in long circles.
sometimes we walk out and then come back the same way.
sometimes we walk in the woods instead of on the roads.
i love to walk in the woods the most.

many times the little master takes me for walks.
the little master does not go as far,
but she runs instead of walks.
i love to run, it feels so good.
when i walk with the little master it is my job to protect her.

we walk first thing in the morning.
even when i am still asleep i must listen for the masters inside the house.
sometimes we start before the sun comes up.
when i see the masters with my big blue leash
it makes me the happiest dog on earth.
i have to sit while they attach my leash.
it is so exciting, that is very hard to do.

after i am on the leash, we go.
the master decides which way we will go that day.
i must concentrate and do a good job.
if i pounce on a toad, or chase a rabbit, or pull too much
master will turn around and we will go home.
master always warns me first.
he tells me, "stick to business, mr big."

sometimes i see nasty cats or buzzards on our territory.
it is very hard, but master will not let me chase them away.

but the hardest thing is when other dogs bark at us while we walk.
it is our territory, and those dogs should not be on it.
especially they should not bark at us on our territory.
master tells me, "stick to business, mr big."

if the dogs get too close master chases them away.
he raises his stick and goes right at them.
i must watch carefully so i do not get in his way.
the other dogs always run.
my master is powerful.

we see cars, trucks, and tractors.
sometimes they stop to talk to master.
if i am lucky, they pet me.

sometimes we see bicycles.
bicycles are very scary,
but master is not afraid of anything.

i have to pay close attention while we walk.
master might tell me to "stop" or "sit" and "wait."
sometimes we do "heel."
when we do "heel" i must walk right beside master's leg
and not go past him.
"heel" is very hard,
but after we do "heel" master always praises me and pets me.

when we get home, master feeds me.
after i eat we sit on the porch and he pets me and talks to me.
then i get to take a long nap in the sun.

i need a good nap, because walk is hard work.
but it is very important.

it is good to have important work to do.

big dog

july 15, 2011
big standards for true ultrarunners

big is the only one with the *true* ultrarunning spirit.
of course, he will probably never run an actual ultra,
he is built like a brick,
overheats if it gets over 50 degrees,
and he still limps from his shot shoulder if we go too far.

but big is always game.
tuesday it was still 90 when we went out for our 4am workout.
he should have been hiding behind his bigloo,
but he was turning flips, rarin' to go.

by the time we got home,
his chin was dragging the ground.
he ran straight to his pool
and splashed himself soaking wet,
before going over and collapsing on the ground.

when i went in, amy was fixin' to go out.
i warned her that big might not be up to any more mileage.

but, when she went out the door with his blue leash
he started doing flips and going nuts, rarin' to go.

when they came back he looked like he'd been run over.
he ran to his pool & splashed like crazy
(i think steam was coming off him)

amy came in & said, "i didn't think he was going to make it.
you never heard such huffing & puffing."

i looked out the window,
and there stood big,
in his pool, head hanging, water dripping off him.

so i asked amy,
"what do you think he would do if i went out there with his blue
leash?"

"there isn't any question... he'd be rarin' to go.
he'd run till he dropped dead, if someone would take him."

others may talk the talk.
big walks the walk.

laz

july 25, 2011
the biggest fear

i don't know why that big ugly dog chose me.
from the day he showed up,
he seems to have made it his life goal to please me.

this dog, whose sad history is evidenced by the things he fears.
his fear of children,
that stemmed from being chained helpless in a yard,
where children gathered to throw rocks at him.

his fear of bicycles, the origin of which i do not know.

his fear of dark skinned men.
his fear of men with sticks,
that reveal so much of the hard times he has known.

why this dog decided to turn to me when he was hurt,
i will never understand.
this dog with every reason to hate people,
whose greatest pleasure is to give & receive affection with them.

i had one regret as i prepared for this year's vol-state.
there was no way for big to come.
his greatest fear is abandonment,
a situation he fully understands.
i only need to work late to be greeted as if i had been given up for
dead.
if i am gone overnight, my loyal friend is too upset to eat.
i wasn't sure how he would handle me being gone for almost two
weeks.

as i went about my race duties
i asked about him every chance i got,
and was relieved to hear that his hunger strike only lasted so
long.
but i was saddened to hear that he had given up on barking for
me to come out in the mornings.

halfway thru the event,
the race passed close enough for me to stop at the house.
altho i came in the middle of the night,
i was greeted as if i had returned from the dead.
the next morning i squeezed in a truncated walk, and fed my
friend, altho he alternated between eating a few bites
and coming over for a reassuring pat.

the rest of my stay was spent doing laundry,
so i would have clothes for the rest of the race,
and packing more supplies.
"facilitating", as carl calls it, "is almost as demanding as running."
(it just doesn't hurt)

when i was getting ready to go, a thunderstorm passed thru.
while i was preparing to head back out on the course,
big stood in the rain, watching,
instead of staying under shelter.
he hates to get rained on, but he has his priorities.

all packed and ready, i made one final stop.
to tell big i was leaving.
as i walked up, big was more excited than ever.
he called out with his loving, "wooo---wooo---wooo"
he leaped in the air, higher than my head,
and performed his famous flips.
big can probably read minds. he seemed to know i was leaving.
as he was leaping and cavorting around,
he misjudged his distance and planted a big muddy paw right in
the middle of my clean white shirt.
cranky, short of sleep, and unworthy of my dog
i flashed anger.
"dangit big, i just washed that shirt."
without thinking i gave him a boot.
not a kick mind you; i just hit him with the side of my foot.
and not very hard.
if it was meant to get his attention, it did.
before my eyes, the big became the deflated.
he quickly sat, a stricken look in his eyes.
i realized he had never been physically punished since he got
here.

i petted him and apologized.
he pressed his soggy body up aginst me,
desperate for reassurance.
we stayed that way a while, but i had duties calling.
eventually i had to go change my shirt & leave.
i stopped by again before i left.
you can bet big didn't jump up on me this time.
as i walked to the car, he watched me go, despondent.

if big spent the rest of the week thinking he had messed up,
and i was gone
(amy said he was sad and needy all week)
i spent the week,
(whenever i wasn't busy)
feeling sorry for my big.
and feeling that i had let him down.

fortunately for me, dogs don't bear grudges.
when i got home in the wee hours of sunday morning,
i was still greeted as a conquering hero.
big got lots of attention thru the next day.
a short walk
another walk, thru the woods
(his first excursion on the backyard trail)
and some sessions with naresh
to begin to alleviate his fear of dark-skinned men.
(i'm not sure how he categorizes naresh,
but big was certainly afraid of him at first).
this morning we got back into our normal routine,
with a 4 am walk.
big didn't make a peep until he saw me coming with his leash.

tomorrow morning i bet he is listening for my eyes to open.

laz

august 01, 2011
the big backyard ultra

ever since we moved to the house in the woods, i have been building trails. last year, while big was gone, we even had a little 11 hour race on the trails i had built.

this year we are planning a new event in big's honor.
we are connecting some of the existing trails to make a 4 mile loop.
it is going to be called the big trail.

the plan for the event is to hold a race around the 4 mile trail at exactly 0700.
then to hold another at exactly 0800...
and 0900...
and every hour, on the hour, until only one person can finish a 4-mile loop.

it will be a different format than any race we have ever heard of, and runners are pretty excited about trying it.
not to mention there is a lot of anticipation for meeting "the big"
everyone has heard about big.

i think there is a perfect irony here.
the race will last until the last man is standing...

a pit bull is staging an event where humans will fight to the "death."

laz

august 04, 2011
Big, medium, and belly rubs

big and little are as different as their names.
when big goes for a walk, he is all business.
he keeps his eyes straight ahead & walks steadily,
right beside me.

little, on the other hand, is all over the place.
her head is on a pivot,
and she is ahead of me, behind me, anywhere & everywhere.

little struts when we pass houses where other dogs live
big is oblivious,
except when he is with amy...
then he is determined that the winston's dog not "threaten" her.
even tho months have passed,
he will apparently never get over that dog acting like it was going
to bite amy.
amy is in pretty good paws when she runs with big.
he takes his job protecting her 100% seriously.

altho big seems to be focused straight ahead,
he is very aware of his surroundings.
the morning after a lister referred to big as a "medium"
i saw amy & big heading out for a run.

unlike other days, i was standing on the back porch.
big walked along, as usual, looking to neither side
until he reached the bottom of the steps to the porch.
there, instead of going past, as he does every other day,
he executed a 90 degree turn,
with military precision,
and came right up the steps to me.
amy, who had been on the other end of a loose leash,
flapped along behind like a pennant.

while big was leaning his head against me for petting
amy regained her balance (and her dignity)
and stated flatly, "*that* is not a medium."

big is just a lot of dog in a very compact space.
as case put it, "it looks like someone made a dog out of a barrel."

that block of muscle design is what allows big to make his
prodigious leaps and flips.
amy got one of those fancy new phones,
and (wanting to be the next carl)
she decided to video big doing flips & post it.
she chose that opportune moment,
case had come to visit & was stopping to see big
big was, of course, jumping about like a crazy dog,
leaps, flips, pirhouettes...

until amy pulled out her phone.
he immediately sat down & posed for her.
(i think he even turned his "best side" to the camera)
recording big's stunts for posterity may take some doing.
who knew he would be so camera conscious?

but then,
who would have guessed that he'd never had a belly rub?
how can any puppy reach doghood
without ever having experienced a belly rub?
being that he is a boy, it is more of a chest rub,
but that doesn't matter.

once amy introduced him to the concept
it didn't take long for him to become an addict.
all it takes is the simple question,
"would you like a belly rub, big?"
and he is over on his back,
his alligator mouth agape in a huge grin.

of course, since his head is upside down,
his big jowls droop "up" exposing an enormous mouth filled with
huge teeth,
in what looks like a vicious snarl
he rolls his eyes up to look at you,
making a large part of the whites show.
it gives him the appearance of a deranged dog-clown.

it is the stuff of nightmares
until you see that big tail wagging back & forth in the dirt.

when big makes his list of the finer things in life.
belly rubs are going to be way up near the top.

laz

august 03, 2011
big dilemma

big didn't get to run this morning.
he got his 4am constitutional with me just fine,
but amy wasn't up to running with him this morning.
the last couple of days he has about pulled her leash arm off.

the problem isn't that big is not serious about his job.
you couldn't ask for a more conscientious worker.
it isn't that he can't learn.
he doesn't even take off after the short hares any more.

the problem is, he is too serious about protecting amy...
and he never forgets.

amy & big have their own special relationship.
amy likes to sit out there with big and read or work crossword
puzzles while big lays there as a living foot-stool.
(from what i hear, he also helps with the hard clues on the
crosswords)
amy introduced big to the carnal pleasure of belly-rubs.
amy takes him out for runs.
amy has that dog wrapped around her little finger.
big would take on an elephant for his amy.

two mornings ago, as amy & big were heading down the road,
mr winston's dog came towards the road, barking.
big has not forgotten the day mr winston's dog threatened to bite
amy.
(that was the first time i ever saw him in "kill" mode)
being a smart dog,
big also remembered he isn't supposed to run in front of us and
under our feet while on the leash...
so he cut behind amy to go take care of the threat.
if any of you ever had a string powered top,
you know what happened when big hit the end of the leash.
i regret that i wasn't there to see the show
(even amy knows it had to look funny)

but it took her 20 yards up mr winston's driveway
(as a human streamer)
before she could convince big to stop.

yesterday morning there were buzzards in the trees down by the
road.
big also remembers the day the buzzard startled amy
(which he perceived as a threat,
the only other time i have seen him in "kill" mode)
so he began running back & forth barking to chase them away.
amy went from being a human top to being a human yo-yo.

when you add in that both mornings,
amy & big met me on the road
(amy accepts that when big sees me, he is going to run to me...
with his amy pennant streaming out behind)
4 draggings in two days
and her leash arm was pretty sore.

she was not impressed by my explanation that having a left arm
2 inches longer than the right would be an asset if she learned
how to pitch left handed.

so this morning big got left out of the rotation...
altho he did his best to remind amy that she needed his help.

big doesn't feel like i need so much protection.
(how can i? i am a god who doesn't even fear bicycles!)
i have ample ballast to stop a charging big,
but never need to use it.
when i am walking him,
he just casts a baleful glare at the winston's dog or the buzzards.

as an aside,
it is a funny thing about big's eyes.
when i first saw him, they looked like demon eyes all the time.
now i can see them shine with joy when people come to see him
i can see them soften with affection when i look into them,
one on one...
and i can see them fill with hate when he is looking at buzzards.
(if big could climb trees, we wouldn't have buzzards)

146

big never forgets.
he considers amy his special charge.
and that is the dilemma.
it is comforting to know that she has such a staunch defender at
her side.
but he may pull her arm off, himself.

laz

august 04, 2011
big's short creek mystery

about 2/3 of the way thru our walk this morning,
big & i found the road completely blocked by a huge fallen tree.
while we were trying to find a way around
we were startled by buzzards taking off...

that's right.
the buzzard tree is down.
the buzzards are just sitting around in the field beside it.

amy & i discussed it,
and i last saw big (attached to his cable)
when i went out & visited him shortly before dark.
and he was on his cable this morning at 4,
when i went out to get him for our walk.
no one can positively account for his whereabouts in between
(about an 8 hour period)

now that i think about it
big did not seem surprised to see the tree across the road.

i'm just saying...

laz

august 09, 2011
The big escape

monday i was feeling a little flat.
maybe that was because big's 4am walk time was less than 12
hours after we left the hotter than snot run in atlanta.
even tho case & i had spent some time making big feel loved
when we got home sunday night,
he was still a little out of sorts about missing his sunday walk...
(NO ONE PATROLLED BIG'S ROAD!!!)
he doubled his usual efforts on doing flips & leaps as i came out.
there was just enough light to see the blaze on his chest
flying thru the darkness
between the thuds of his feet hitting the ground.

after big had "sat"
(actually vibrated across the ground on his backside)
and got his leash on,
we started to walk.
two steps in, big pounced on a toad.

i couldnt see the toad, because it was dark.
but i know big's toad pounce.
i have been trying to discourage toad pouncing
because it is hard on the toads.
rat pouncing is allowed... encouraged even
because it is hard on the rats.
i know it isn't a rat pounce when big doesn't grab the victim.
he only ever picked up one toad (the first one) with his mouth.

this seemed like the perfect day to reinforce the no toad
pouncing rule.
"ok big. that's it. you know better than to bother the toads"
i turned around, put him back on his cable.
then we did the feeding and watering routine before i moved on
to take care of little.
big wasn't too happy.
it was even worse because amy wasn't home to take him
running.

after little and i did our morning routine
and i was getting ready to take a shower
i heard sandra holler, "big is out of his collar!"
i put my shorts back on and went to look out the window.
sure enough, big's cable lay there
attached to nothing but an empty collar.
i was immediately concerned...
"i better go find big before someone shoots him!"
but when i went to the back door,
there was the big looking in at me,
wagging his tail,
a monstrous grin splitting his head in half,
and a mischievous gleam in his eye.

when i opened the door,
i was braced to catch him coming in
(it's kind of like catching a hairy cannonball)
but instead of bursting in,
he ran down the steps and partway down our walking trail
before turning and looking back at me,
"come on, we have a walk to do!"
"not today big, c'mone"
he knows c'mone (come on)
he hesitated and looked down the trail, then back at me,
"but who's keeping an eye on the buzzards?"
(the buzzards have found them a new tree)
"how do i know some nasty cat hasn't been walking on my road?"
"naw, not today. c'mone big fella"
with that he trotted back to me.

when we got to his cable, the issue with the collar was clear.
it has a complicated latching mechanism
which keeps him from slipping it over his head,
yet allows it to be loose enough that he can breathe.
the latch had been opened large enough to fit an elephant.
it took me a few minutes to figure out how to fit it back to big
size.

i'm not as good with latches as big...
i am limited by wanting them to still work when i get done.

152

now i am left to wonder;
did big just get lucky,
or has he figured that thing out.

this turn of events certainly reopens the question about exactly
what happened to the old buzzard tree...

mr winston said he saw it happen.
right in the middle of the big lightning storm a huge explosion
took down the tree.
mr winston is pretty sure it was a lightning strike.
i am wondering where ben stores the fertilizer for his bean
fields...

laz

august 15, 2011
Big backyard ultra update

all 40 slots have been claimed.
the first-come part of the event is done,
but i might take one or two additional entries
(to allow for drops or no-shows)
if someone with potential to contend applies.
now that i'm unemployed i worry more about the backyard
budget, as there will be no cash infusions from laz!
a couple more entries would be comforting.
(and a couple more contenders would add to the bloodbath)

tim came up and did some trailwork saturday.
he was a human dynamo.

we now have a good half mile of the trail thoroughly "groomed"
(2 miles to go-1.5 out/back with a 1 mile loop on the end)
when i commented on how darn thorough tim was,
he replied, "i have to run on this thing... for a loooong time!"

we had a good chance to speculate on strategy.
tim brought up a concern about getting too cooled off between
laps.
i hadn't thought of that.

little helped us all morning.
when we accidentally threw sticks off the trail,
she brought them back for us.

so when we took a break,
tim had to come up to the house & meet big as well.
now big & tim are old friends.

while we were out there making introductions,
sandra came out to make sure tim knew i was looking for a good
home for big.
big & little had been playing their chasing game,
which meant that tim & i had been playing high stakes jump-rope
with big's cable.

as sandra came walking across the big lot,
they started another round, "LOOK OUT!"

sandra is not that good at high stakes jump rope.

i think *the question* is probably coming up again:
"how hard are you trying to find a home for that dog?"

we finished the day a couple of hundred feet from the cutoff to
my front door
so, after i recovered a bit & made my weekly trip to the dump,
i finished the trail on to the cutoff,
and then did the side trail right up to the front steps
(which are about 50 feet from the big trail)
that way i have a nice cleared loop to do.

as i came stob chopping out of the woods
sandra was standing on the porch with a question,
"what are you going to do; run them right thru the house?"
"they'll take their shoes off."

i'm not sure sandra is looking forward to the race as much as i
am.

in case anyone is interested,
i'm planning more trailwork this weekend.

laz

august 22, 2011
bad life choices

after big's run yesterday
i was out there giving him a little affection
(big loves his affection)
when i noticed the tell-tale ridge of a mole tunnel coming out of
the woods.

with only a few meanders it made its way right to the beginning
of the bare ground that marks the edge of big's space.
there it ended...

at a hole, surrounded by loose dirt.
"did you have a visitor mr big?"

big just grinned, and rolled over for a belly rub.
amy opined that the mole just made a "bad life choice."

laz (can identify with the mole)

august 27, 2011
big in training

big has been working hard to prepare to host his own ultra.
earlier this summer he had been getting a little flabby.
having limited time,
both big & little to work with,
and unable to actually run,
i wasn't getting big the amount of work he needed.

now that amy has pitched in to help,
big has been making good progress.
he reached a milestone today,
his first 5 mile day.
once the weather finally cools down a little
big will probably match that total with ease.
but, with his block of muscle physique
and the cooling system of a dog
he has a hard time in temperatures above 50f.

in the midst of the summer heat
5 miles was a worthy challenge.

amy took him out first for a 3 miler.
when they got back,
she warned me that he might not be ready to go again.
(he had to walk the last mile and was pretty beat)
but big is nothing if he isn't willing.
he was in his above-ground pool trying to cool off,
when he saw me come out with his blue leash.
he was out in a flash
leaping about with excitement & doing his flips.

he was, as usual, vibrating like the energizer bunny
while i hooked him up.
and he started out with enthusiasm.
but the heat around here just wont let up
(it reached 100f just yesterday, and i can't remember when it last
got below 70)
he was soon into the big death march mode.

his ability to tough it out would be the envy of any ultrarunner.
my steady pace doesn't seem to be natural for a dog.
big would lag behind, then trot to catch up.
i tried to keep him in the shade as much as possible
but i was sweating myself, even in the shade.
the sunny stretches were rough.

when we got back in the shady stretches
i would stop to let him cool down a bit.
even the short hares
(doing their usual best to make him misbehave)
didn't get much more than a hate stare.

when we got back it was the first time i have seen him wag his
tail because his walk was over.
he went straight to his pool.
ever the big, when he saw me 15 minutes later he was looking
for the leash.
he'd walk 'til he dropped dead if i asked him to.

i've been taking him out on his trail sometimes.
he wants to be ready to lead a guided walk of the course
on friday before the big race.
big loves the trails.
he leads the way, as the chief rattlesnake scout
and his uncanny ability to follow trail would also be the envy of
any ultra-runner.
somehow he can see where the trail went a year ago,
even tho it has been unused all summer and he has never seen it
before.

when we come to places that the trail has been straightened
he will automatically follow the old trail.
(once he is shown the new route he remembers it perfectly)
i wish i could take him on the trails every day
but if i don't spray my feet & legs i get chiggers something
terrible
(if i do spray, i still get a lot, but i can live with them)
& i can't afford to spray down every day.
when we come to the rock ledges
big waits while i climb up (or down)

160

then he will follow with a single bound.
that block of muscle physique may not be effective in heat,
but he can jump 5 feet up onto a rock ledge from a standing start
with graceful ease.
bigs are phenomenal athletes.

during our walks i tell big about the race and the runners who
are coming.
i tell him about the mail he has been getting from all over the
country.
he doesn't ever answer.
but if i think he isn't listening to every word,
all i have to do is tell him to "stop"
(or ask him if he wants a belly rub).

i don't think he understands anything but his commands.
he is, after all, just a dog.
but then i will look out & there he stands at the back door,
grinning...
and he has removed his "dogproof" collar,
or unlatched his "dogproof" cable.

i've never had a dog quite like the big.

and he is training hard for his race.
i think he wants to look his best for the ladies.

laz

September 04, 2011
big fears and superstitions

as smart as big is,
he succumbs to the same superstition as every other dog i have
ever had.
big believes that by pressing his nose against his leash,
somehow it will become connected to his collar.

this is an important belief for big,
because being on the leash is his great love in life.
the only thing better than being on his leash is being petted.

in the world of big, food comes in a distant third.
love, work, and food. that is the big order of priority.

you guys know how the game unfolds.
i come out of the house & start towards the big homestead.
big greets me with his, "wooo---wooo---wooo"
i hold up my hand to show him the big blue leash.
"look what i got, big!"
big goes nuts, leaping & doing flips...

one day last week, big blew a flip and landed flat on his back.
it made me wince to see/hear him hit the hard ground,
but he jumped right back to his feet.
it must have made an impression (or at least left him sore),
because it was a couple of days before he started doing flips
again.

anyway, once i get close, i tell him,
"you have to sit bigness. you gotta be under control."
he sits immediately
(although he can't stop vibrating with excitement)
then i have to maneuver around him & get him back from the
very end of his cable.
otherwise there isn't any slack to take it off.
it isn't that easy, with a vibrating big scooting about on his butt
trying to stay in front of me.

it is during this little dance that (given the opportunity)
big will press his nose against the leash
and then hop to his feet, ready to go.
"it doesn't work that way big"
laughing, i show him the leash.
"you have to sit"
he gives me a look that says, "i put it on, why did you take it off?"
but he sits again.

it still amazes me to think back to when big first showed up,
16 months ago.
i had heard the same stories about these dogs that everyone
hears.
it isn't that i don't still treat them with respect.
the capacity to do damage is so great.
and so many of them have been treated so inappropriately.
any sensible person proceeds with caution.
but the picture of an animal that can turn vicious without
warning is so wrong.

big is a tremendous communicator.
most dogs are.
but people tend to lack the perception to understand what dogs
are telling them.
dogs bark, growl, and make other sounds,
but most of the real communication is thru body language.
people consciously communicate thru sounds,
but we also give off signals with our body language,
and dogs are very good at reading them.
(they don't smell your fear, they see it)

during yesterday's walk me & big ran into any number of things
that used to frighten him to the point he was difficult to control.
vehicles passed, and he never flinched.
even a big log truck went by, crowding into our lane.
all big did was scoot over until he was bumping my legs.
just after we had turned from millersburg onto loop road,
a bicycle came out behind us.
big & the cyclist exchanged looks, but big kept walking.
the bike turned the other way
(possibly because the cyclist wasn't crazy about riding past big)

164

big did keep looking over his shoulder,
in case another bike came,
until we turned onto a different road.
another bike passed us, and big paid it little attention,
and i learned something new about big and bicycles.
he is only afraid of bikes when they are coasting.
the second bike was going on a steady uphill grade,
and the rider had to peddle all the way past us.
the first bike had to stop at an intersection, and coasted to a stop.
to big, a bicycle making the coasting sound is as ominous as a
rattlesnake's rattle.
it makes sense.
cyclists can't peddle and assault innocent pit bulls at the same
time.

anyway, thinking about how big & i have worked on his fears
it struck me how many people talk about their dogs' fears,
and inability to get past them.
if we are preparing our dog to coach us
(like coach big)
we need to get them past the things that frighten them
and disrupt our training program.

our failure to understand how to communicate with our animals
(in my mind)
is a real handicap in dealing with a dog's fears.
we want to reassure and comfort the dog,
as we would with a child.
what we don't think about is that the words have little meaning
to the dog.
by our actions we instead confirm the dog's belief that there is a
reason to be afraid.

with big, i always started by trying to ignore the fearful stimulus,
and go on about our business.
if big starts reacting to the fear instead,
i will scold him a little & try to get him back on track.
if that fails, i make him sit, and stay,
position myself where he has to look at me instead
and focus his attention on me & his commands

even if it means taking his head & turning it so he has to look at me.
if all else fails, we turn & go home
to try again tomorrow.
just like everything else,
it takes patience and consistency to get the results we want.
as always, i stand ready to be corrected by the dog training pros on the list,
but this is what works for me.

laz

part 6: assimilation

the lady master

hello. my name is big and i am a contented dog.
i have everything a dog could want.
i have a master.
i have a family .
i have important work to do.
i have a cozy bigloo.

and i get lots of petting.
master pets me a lot.
he pets me before i eat
he pets me when i do good on a walk
sometimes he just comes out to see me and pets me.
and the best time is in the morning after i have done my work and eaten;
i sit between the master's feet and lean against him while he pets me.

little master pets me a lot.
sometimes when it is warm she brings her chair.
then i lie there while she puts her feet on me and reads.

people who visit come out to pet me.
people who stop in cars while we walk pet me.
people pet me everywhere i go.
the only person who never petted me was the lady master.

i know the lady master likes me.
at first she didn't like me.
she was afraid of me.
after she got to know me she liked me.
but she never talked to me
and she never petted me.

then one day we had a lot of company.
i was doing my job as the dog.
i was being polite and getting petted.
it is very important to be polite.
i cannot jump on people, or push my nose against them.

i cannot stare at them.
i am supposed to stand there quietly
and wait to see if they want to pet me.

the lady master was there.
i always include the lady master if she is there.
but she had never petted me.

this day was different.
i was waiting patiently,
and then she leaned over and stroked my head.
it was the best feeling ever.
when i got to master, he leaned over and whispered in my ear.
then i was sure it was important.

the lady master petted me.
and i am a contented dog.

big dog

september 05, 2011
big fears and superstitions (part 2)

> From: Amy
>
> I'd like to add that Big believes part of Big's job is being aware of whether or not a person makes me nervous while we're running. We go past roadworkers, bikers, etc. with no problem but he always seems to study me just to be sure.

we already know how big responds to a visitor that amy is "uncomfortable" with...

hackles up, ears down, teeth bared, legs stiff...

the growling/barking is superfluous to getting the big message across.

a lot of people are frightened by big's normal appearance,
but when it is actually time to be afraid
he communicates it very clearly.

the funny thing was,
amy disguised her feelings from the other humans that were present, who couldn't figure out, "what came over big?"

whether it is running on our secluded roads,
or being alone at night,
amy feels very safe with big on duty.

laz (who also likes it when amy has big on duty)

September 06, 2011
The big risk

as i write this there is a big red dog on the back porch,
curled up on a ratty old sleeping bag/dog bed behind the back
porch fireplace,
warm and dry, contentedly asleep.

a kind hearted soul has offered to provide the big with a new
(sturdy) bigloo, but it has not yet arrived.

and the weather has done what it does best in tennessee.
it has sabotaged us.
on saturday big was suffering in 102 degree heat
(and splashing his way thru gallons & gallons of water in his
pool.)
sunday it was 98.
but sunday night the rains came.

they continued all day yesterday, with temperatures in the 50s.
and all night last night.
today it added 25 mph winds to the mix.

we brought big up on the porch a few times
dried him off and gave him lots of love.
but a 50 degree swing in temperatures,
with less and less way to stay dry,
that is tough on anybody.

in addition, he was dying to go to work.
we hadn't missed a day walking in several months.

this morning he couldnt stand it any more.
as soon he heard my eyes open he started barking to go.
when i didn't take him he quit barking.
but he just stood there in the freezing cold rain.

finally i couldn't stand it any more
so i brought him up on the porch & made him a bed.
i figure he can't possibly wander off in this mess...

173

whether that is true remains to be seen.
i already had to retrieve him once.

he'll definitely have to be put back in big country when the rain
stops and i hope no one "shows up" at the house while he is
loose.
he isn't going to hurt anyone,
but he scares the pee out of people when he is on his cable.
i don't want to think of their response if he comes running up
loose,
even if he only wants to say hello!

it just isn't right to have big tied up out there
with no place dry to take refuge.
so it is a calculated risk.
i am keeping an eye on him
because i am trapped here anyway,
waiting on a call about a job that i expect to come any time.

hope his bigloo arrives soon!

laz (oh heck, there he goes again!)

September 06, 2011
The big risk (part 2)

> From: lazarus lake
> [...]
> laz (oh heck, there he goes again!)

and from there came another big adventure.

amy & i had been keeping an eye on the big.
(his sleep to trouble time is 1.024 seconds)

while i was out of the room,
he got up & decided it was time for some action.
amy called out, "big is on the move again."
"he's looking in the door."
"he's going to mark the post... NO BIG NO!"
"i was in time; he's going to pee in the yard."
"he's headed around front. he's trying to find you."

in just a moment i saw his big head looking in the window.
"big, you gotta stay on the porch"

big gave me a look that said, "we are supposed to go walk!"
i started to put on my boots to go out & try to convince him to
stay settled.
"he's at the back door again."
"wait. i think he's leaving."

i was hopping around trying to get the second boot on.
why is everything always difficult when you are in a hurry?
"he's heading down the driveway."

finally getting my boots tied,
i grabbed my jacket & went out the back door;
"BIG... BIG... C'MONE BOY."

i knew calling would be useless.
he'd been wanting to go for his walk since yesterday.
he'd given up on me, and didn't give a darn about the rain.

he was ready to go.
now, big learns most commands with but a single repetition
(it is uncanny)
but come when called (c'mone)...
he still thinks that is the order to play "catch me if you can"

grabbing my little umbrella i headed down the driveway in the
pouring rain, as fast as i could go.

i rightly figured he would stick to our regular routes.
thank god; i could never have found him otherwise,
and i was in a race against big getting himself shot.

as i came in sight of the road,
i saw him go past the end of the driveway at a dead run,
"BIG STOP, BIG COME BACK HERE. BIIIIG"

big never broke stride,
leaving me to ponder what he'd been managed to do in the past 2
minutes, "oh great, he's been to the neighbors' house with cats."
(geez, big hates cats)
i could only hope he hadn't eaten one
(no one has called, so maybe we're good.
cats aren't likely to be out in the rain)

as i chugged around the corner in the direction big had
disappeared i heard the winston's dogs start barking.
i could see them long before i got around the corner to the end of
their drive, and both dogs were looking down the driveway,
barking furiously.

in just a moment
big's unmistakable red figure came into view.
he was running straight at them, still at top speed.

i stopped and watched as the gap between big and disaster
closed with frightening swiftness.
but the winston's dogs are no fools.
when big had closed within 50 yards,
they hightailed it for the porch.
not that it was any better place to die.

176

apparently scattering them was sufficient response to their
having threatened amy,
because big thundered over to the spot they'd been standing
marked their own vantage point as big territory with a flourish
then took back off,
made a sweeping turn and disappeared down the hill into the
pasture without breaking stride.

i experienced a short lived relief,
"thank god he didn't take out the dogs... oh crap, THE COWS!"
with a touch of despair, i cranked it back up,
heading towards where big had vanished.
i am just so slow, there is no telling what he would do before i
could get there.

as i came to the place the winston's dogs had abandoned
big came flying up the hill out of the woods
(from a completely different direction than he had disappeared)
he stopped about 20 feet away,
soaking wet, huffing and puffing like a steam engine
and looked over at the dogs cowering on the porch.

then he looked at me,
and i swear that silly son of a gun was grinning.
"big. you come here right now."
i showed him his leash and he trotted over without hesitation
and then stood there, panting & drenched,
while i attached it.
"you darn fool. you are going to get yourself shot again."
he just gave me that same grin, his eyes twinkling with mischief.
he seemed to be saying,
"you needed to get off your lazy butt and do something today."

what can you do?
i laughed at him, and we started for home.

the rest of the walk was as unremarkable as any other day
(except it was pouring rain on us)
when we got to the house there was no bed on the porch for big.
instead, he is back in his swamp.

at least the old bigloo pedestal was fairly dry up under his tarp roof.
as i type this, he is sleeping on it peacefully...
rain or no rain.

i sure as heck hope the rain stops by tomorrow.
big needs something constructive to do.
because he is going to do *something*

laz

september 09, 2011
team big

the big set a new pr today
(now that the weather is cooling off some)

eight miles.

he looked invincible until the sun came out after about 7.

he was wiped when we got home,
but an hour later he was ready to go again.

he wants you to know he has his sights set on an ultra this year.

laz

september 09, 2011
buddy and pretty girl-big and his peer group

buddy is an idiot...

or an evil genius.

buddy is ben's dog & lives at the next farm down the road.
buddy is a golden retriever,
and big assures me that those are not the smartest dogs on earth.
buddy is a lucky dog.
ben has some rental properties in murfreesboro
and after one of his tenants left
when ben went to clean up the house,
there was buddy.
now buddy is here.

it is bad news for big's walk when buddy sees us.
he comes out to the road, and walks 20 yards in front of us.
this is unbearable to big.
big is the number one dog.
and he certainly was not meant to follow a mentally challenged
golden retriever.
big, eyes fixed on buddy's tail, subtly increases his pace
until he is pulling me down the road. "big... BIG. SLOW DOWN!"
big drops back beside me sheepishly.
then, 60 seconds later he is gradually pulling ahead again.

big & i had a nice 5 miler planned for this morning.
but, who should we run into at the bottom of the first hill but
buddy.
buddy just stood there & waited until we were about 20 yards
away, then he started walking in front of us.

big & i began our routine. "big... BIG. SLOW DOWN!"
"that's better, don't pay any attention to buddy. he is an idiot."...
"big...BIG. SLOW DOWN!"

i was hoping buddy would turn in at his own driveway,
but he went right past.

i stopped, & put big thru his paces,
so buddy would move on ahead.
buddy stopped & waited.

buddy is an idiot.
or an evil genius.

after a mile & a half
big & i finally just turned around and went home.
amy can verify; it is not feasible to walk big if he pulls.
he will pull your arm out of its socket.

as soon as we turned, big was his usual self.
the rest of the workout was pleasant...
but big likes to get in his miles & today he got cut short.

had we gone the other direction,
we would not have seen pretty girl.
pretty girl is another pit.

she is not a lucky dog, like buddy.
she was also abandoned in murfreesboro,
but she ended up in the hands of the boy (early 20s) that lived in
the cabin.
he attached pretty girl to a chain in front of his house,
and there she was.

one day, when she had first arrived,
i heard her crying piteously as i came walking down the road.
when i got to the cabin
the boy and his wife were sitting on the front porch.
pretty girl was at the end of her chain,
as close to them as she could get,
begging for some attention.
i wanted to cry.

at first, when i walked past,
pretty girl would charge to the end of her chain
lunging, snarling, growling, and barking ferociously...
acting just like a vicious pit bull is supposed to act.
i didn't know her name, so i started calling her pretty girl.

"hello pretty girl
i know your secret.
i know you aren't a mean dog.
you just need some lovin', don't you"

every time i went by,
i would stop & talk to pretty girl for a few minutes.
i don't reckon it was productive for me & the sizes' training,
but after a while,
pretty girl started to wag her tail when she came out.

she quit hitting the end of her chain like a runaway train.
the crazy barks turned to greeting barks.
a lonesome dog is grateful for any affection it can get.
i always promised her, "one of these days, when i don't have a
dog with me, i'm gonna come up there & pet you."

and then, a few days ago
the cabin was empty, and pretty girl was gone.
i wont ever know how her story ends,
but i hope she ends up in a better place.

you are supposed to go pet your dog now.
i know i did.

laz

september 13, 2011
big discipline

i still think big could have chosen better when he picked out a
master. he needs someone with more time.
right now he is out back hollering at amy to finish up running
with the inferior dog (sophie),
and come take him for a run.

the road she runs passes the house at the bottom of the hill.
it is about a quarter mile away thru the woods,
but big can hear your footsteps when you walk past.
so big lets you know both leaving the house,
and a half mile later walking past the bottom of the hill,
that he is "READY TO GO!"

after amy finishes with him,
i'll be taking him out for a 5 miler.
8 mile days aren't routine for the big ...

yet.

but, as the weather cools & he keeps getting in better shape,
the outcome is inevitable.
it is hard to keep a dog this intelligent from getting bored.
and more exercise just works until he gets in better shape.

with our expanding range it has become necessary that big deal
with lots of other dogs on the run.
unlike amy, i can't mentally handle lots of short out & backs.
Me & big like to go places and see things.
i didn't have any idea how to prepare big for the dogs we would
meet,
tennessee is famous in some circles for the number of simply
loose undisciplined dogs.
little has never mastered staying calm when dogs come after us.
i have to control her with one hand
while preparing to use my dog trainer on any dog that ventures
too close with the other
(something they only do once)

but little has issues with too much stimulation
she is a smart dog, but cannot control herself when she overloads
(have i ever mentioned that anyone crossing a jack russell with a
bull terrier should receive the death penalty?)

i would not want any part of trying to handle big out of control.
instead of trying to stave off another dog,
i would be trying to save its life.

once we started ranging further afield my worries were greatly
assuaged.
big is not little.
for one thing, far fewer dogs seem anxious to come out in the
road & challenge big.
either the optical illusion that he is larger than he actually is
extends to dogs as well as people,
or the reputation of pit bulls does the same.
maybe both.
and the other difference is that big does not have the issues with
self control.

our first test was with lynnor's pug
(why don't you come get that irritating little mutt, lynnor?)
90% of the dogs we see come running toward the road barking,
big just turns his head & gives them a look.
then they stop, shut up, and watch us pass by.
some continue barking,
few come out in the road.
none of those have actually threatened us yet...
except lynnor's retarded pug.

lynnor's pug is incapable of learning.
lynnor blasted him with pepper spray,
ben has smacked him with a stick,
i have seen other dogs whip his silly tail,
and big could swallow him whole.
he still charges out to attack anything that passes.

the first time, big wanted to respond.
we did the routine. "sit" "stay" "look at me" "get under control"

186

big seemed to immediately understand that he was to ignore
lynnor's pug,and has never responded to him since...
except for the hair standing on end in a 4 inch strip from his neck
to his tail.

the next big test was the trailer dog.
big test for both of us,
as trailer dog attacks buddy every time ben runs that way,
and tries to attack little when we walk past.

trailer dog raised cain, but the big effect was in play.
even trailer dog didn't want a piece of big.

i wonder if the lack of response from my muscled up friend,
except for the pug, he doesn't even raise his hackles,
just that *look* is maybe even more intimidating than if he acted
fierce?

so we have been walking all over.
problem dogs are no problem.

but it would be misleading to say that big does not respond in
any way.
after we walk calmly past some barking idiot,
especially the ones that come out in the road behind us
and fill the air with their hollow threats,
about 100 feet down the road i let big go off and mark a spot.
(i also have learned; i have learned this is important to big...and i
think he deserves it)

he makes his mark,
then without looking back he kicks up great clods of dirt & grass
with all four feet, flinging it back in the direction of the nattering
cur. up until then, you would think he had scarcely noticed.
after he comes back on the road, and we continue.
i half expect him to look up at me & wink.

if big was a person,
he'd be the guy you'd want to have around in a crisis.

laz

september 17, 2011
big day in the backyard

i just love a backyard where there is always something new.

big's list family had lots of good suggestions for his boredom issue.
he is due a new chew bone.
i've shopped around looking for one too big for little to steal.
little is a skillful thief.

big loves his chew bones,
but he doesn't get to enjoy them for long.
big chews joyously for a while, then leaves the bone lying about.
little comes out of nowhere, at 90 miles an hour,
deftly snatches big's bone right out from in front of him,
before he can leap to his feet and launch a futile pursuit.

later i find big's chew bone wherever little abandons it
(usually on the other end of the house)
and return it to him
that way he can chew on it joyously for a while and then leave it
lying about so the process can be repeated.

big isn't a particularly toy oriented dog.
he likes toys, but doesn't play with them much.
besides, little steals them.
i got him a red bone.
we play with it sometimes (for maybe 5 minutes)
for big, toys seem to be less about play than ownership.
he had a red bone before, he liked to lay beside it in the sun.
but little always stole it.
now he has a big house, and a new red bone.
he put the red bone in his house.
little can't snatch it, because there is no escape route.

josh's suggestion to teach him tricks was a great one.
except i realized i don't know any dog tricks
(much less how to teach them)
big doesn't show any natural ability as a hunting dog,

or we would work on that.
what big loves most is running (or walking)
and his favorite place to walk is the trails in the back yard.

little has been the only one who gets to accompany me on my
work days on the trail.
little knows how to stay close (and not kill animals)
sometimes she stays a bit too close
after she tires of playing in the woods,
and running 90 miles an hour back & forth up the trail,
she likes to lie down beside the next stob slated for chopping.

today was different.
today i was doing a job which big could come along.
over the summer a number of trees had fallen across the trail.
since my chain saw is out of commission,
but i still have plenty of sweat,
today was slated for clearing the trees with a hand saw.

amy had already taken him out to run a few miles,
but when big saw his blue leash in my hand he started jumping
up & down with excitement.
he would kill in the backyard format, because he is never too
tired to get excited about going again.
when we turned onto the trail instead of going to the road,
he was overjoyed.

big has a great trail trick that he taught himself.
when little is on leash on the trail,
sometimes we go on opposite sides of a tree.
naturally, we both hit the end of the leash at the same time
and little strains to continue, while choking herself,
until i pass the leash around the tree so we can continue.
big seldom takes the wrong side of a tree.
if he does, he backs up and comes around on my side.
the reason he seldom goes the wrong way is that he sees them
coming.

when he spots one, i can see him looking at me, to see which way
i am going to go.
then he follows.
190

so we walked around the whole loop today.
we'd walk along until we came to a downed tree.
then i'd hook big's leash on a branch & saw the downed tree
apart.
i made a point of asking big for his opinion of how to approach
each tree.

big enjoys being talked to.
he listens with that solemn expression of his,
and i think he feels important.
(heck, i'm not sure he doesn't understand)

since i only had a handsaw, a couple of larger trees, i only sawed
off enough limbs so the trunk would lie flat on the trail.
(those will rot enough to completely remove in a couple of years
and they'll be easy to jump... at least for a while)

when we took a rest break,
big sat leaning against my leg.
we listened to the sounds of the woods.
watched the wind in the trees
and were a contented pair.

the only time big had difficulty was in the northeast corner of the
property where the deer bed down.
fresh deer tracks were all over the trail, and judging from big's
nose action there was plenty of scent as well.

it's hard not to pull on the leash when you have an overwhelming
desire to run down a deer.
(maybe big has some hunting in his blood after all)

it took several hours before we reached the end of the cleaned
trail, and then we went on. big & i decided we wanted to get all
the sawing behind us in one day.

one tangle, where 3 trees came down together, took a long time
to clear, and we had to move the trail a little ways to one side.

another spot, we saw a way to remove a big dogleg, and shorten
the trail.

at the wobbly rocks, where the cut-through is to connect,
we scouted around and found a way to enter one of the mini-
canyons.

big agreed that it would be so cool to run down during the race.
it was well worth all the dadgum sawbriers we went thru
(the ones me & little will remove before the race)

then we came to a decision point.
i hadn't ever been over the whole route of the cut-through.
there was a cross fence that i had walked down partway from
either end, but i hadn't been all the way thru.
going thru briery woods with no trail is hard work on a leash
(either end).
big was obviously tired already,
but he was game to go on.

i am glad we did.
the cross fence doesn't go all the way thru,
and we had to guess at our route. (for a memphis squirrel hunter
this might have taken several days)

we had quite an adventure.
found an open marsh that i never knew existed,
right in the middle of the woods.
we followed part of a creekbed that i hadn't been down before,
and even found a small grassy meadow out in the woods.
i just love a backyard where there is always something new.

big was challenged to his utmost,
keeping his leash from getting tangled on small trees and in the
briers.
my hand saw was less than useless, leaving me no free hand,
but we had a blast.
by the time we came walking up the trail to the house,
we were both whipped.
but when i hooked big back on his cable, he looked up at me
and when i looked in his eyes i could hear my kids when they
were small, "this was the best day ever!"
does it make up for the times i had to (and hopefully will have to
again) work late?

192

or the days it rains and he never gets to come out from under his tarp?
i can't tell you.
but today big was one happy dog.

i started for the house, and then looked back.
big went and took a long drink,
then went over to his favorite sunny spot and lay down with a huge sigh.

it was a big day in the backyard

laz

september 20, 2011
big gratitude

yesterday could have been another terrible day for big.
it started good.
amy took him out for 3 miles of running,
and i started out with him on a 2 mile walk...

but it started to rain on us.
big channeled charlie brown,
"this is just a passing shower... we can still walk"
but i already knew the forecast.
we headed on home.

last time it rained all day was miserable for everyone.
big was either stuck sitting in his bigloo rubble,
standing in the rain barking his "HELP ME!" bark,
or just laying in the mud, looking depressed.
we brought him up on the porch a few times to dry off
and get loved on,
but he wouldn't stay put by himself and no one could sit with
him all day.

yesterday he had his new donated big house.
it even has an old sleeping bag inside...

another tribute to big's smarts.
little & sophie can only have straw.
they love cloth bedding when it is cold,
but the first time it is nice they drag it out & tear it to shreds.
big drug his out once.
i put it back & told him to leave it there,
and there it has been ever since.

so, anyway, all day yesterday
big was in his house.
mostly he slept, sometimes he looked out the door at the rain.
he never barked.
he was reluctant to even come out to eat
(in the dry space under his tarp)

big loves his new house.
so big is grateful
and so are the people who live with him.
it is gutwrenching to see him miserable,
and be unable to fix it for him.

he did a nice run & walk this morning
had a good breakfast
then he got a nice chicken treat
which he ran in circles shaking and throwing and chasing down
until it was thoroughly covered with mud.
then he ate it.
and now he is laying in the sun...
content.

big thanks you.
lots of dogs like big do not have happy lives
and big's life certainly got off to a rocky start.
but thanks to his many friends, he is a happy dog.

laz

september 23, 2011
big & shirtless men

in a related matter...

one of big's issues from his previous life is men without shirts.
(just watch any episode of "cops" & you'll get an idea why)

he loves carl,
but when carl finished running & went to say hello to big without
a shirt on, big was very leery.

however, we don't know if big is disturbed by women with no
shirt...
but i would allow an experiment, just so we'll know.
i am even willing to be on hand as a safety precaution.

laz

september 26, 2011
the antibig

each dog has their own character.
at our house, the big, with his big personality, tends to
overshadow his peers.
but they have their own unique qualities as well.
sophie, with her goofy grin & her chow-hound approach to life,
has acquired the nickname "the anti-big"

big is almost scary with his houdini-like escape ability.
we long ago gave up enclosing him in any pen or cage.
there doesn't seem to be a latch invented that he cannot defeat.
and if worse comes to worst,
he simply goes thru the walls that enclose him.

during his indoor days in st louis,
he got a reputation for being able to open doors.
and when they tried locking him in,
he simply took the door off its hinges.
chain link fence? not a problem.
he can make holes in chain link fence
by unraveling it where it attaches.

we have a tentative truce about being on a cable.
he mostly stays on it, but if he feels like things are out of hand,
such as when it rained for 2 days and he didn't have a house.
or this weekend, when amy didn't take him running on
consecutive days,
he just takes off his dog-proof collar,
or unfastens his dog-proof cable
(a feat that requires both of my hands),
and comes looking for us.

amy had taken sophie running this morning,
sophie always runs first,
while big barks his complaints about amy taking the inferior dog.
but this morning i went out on the porch, thinking big was
unusually quiet.
then i heard amy & sophie coming up the drive.

but what came around the corner was not amy & sophie,
it was big... collarless.
not intending to be left out again, he had taken off his collar and
gone to look for amy.
my plans to save up money for a 5-foot, extra-strength, chain link
fence took a blow
when big saw me, and casually jumped up onto the 5 foot high
porch,
without even gathering himself.
now i suppose i need to test him on a 6 foot barrier.

sophie & little inherited the big pen.
we flipped the panels over, so the big holes were at the top,
and sophie & little have a place outside to stay when we are gone
or the weather is nice.
one day i came home to find that we had forgotten to latch the
door that morning.
it would open with the slightest push.
sophie & little were standing inside waiting for someone to let
them out.
(amy assures me that sophie is simply too polite to escape)

when big is with amy, he considers himself her protector.
anything new along the route, he has to check out.
any threat, like a barking dog, a passing vehicle, or the buzzards,
he gets between her and it.
sophie picks her enemies more judiciously.
a few weeks ago, someone dumped an old gas tank in the
entrance to mr robbins' property.
each morning, when they pass it, sophie stretches herself up as
tall as she can get,
& growls fiercely at the hunk of metal.
(amy defends her pup with claims that the gas tank sometimes
changes position during the night)
more threatening foes, such as anything that is not inanimate,
sophie counts on amy protecting her.

big likes other dogs.
they need to understand that he is the number one dog,
but he is otherwise very friendly with them...
or ignores them when he is on the job.

200

he plays a frightening game with little.
they meet in the air, looking like mortal combat between a giant and a midget,
with big growling ferociously
and little emitting her distinctive war cry
(it sounds something like a pack of coyotes being run thru a thresher)
he will knock her down, step on her, grab her by the throat.
it is hard to watch, because it doesn't seem like he could keep from killing her,
but she always escapes unscathed and comes back for more.

sophie lets every dog know that, "i am not dominant"
when big as much as looks in her direction,
she rolls onto her back.
she roughhouses with little,
even pushes little around sometimes.
because little is the smaller dog...
a fearless (or brainless) dog, but the smaller dog.

little is a shameless thief, dashing thru big's area and snatching his toys or bones as big leaps to his feet a second too late to stop the much quicker little.
then little hides big's things for me to find and return later.

sophie had apparently taken note of this trick.
the other day, big had left his red bone out.
he'd been playing with it, and hadn't put it back in his house to be safe from little.
sophie spotted it, and took off.
as she raced into big's territory, big leapt to his feet.
sophie attempted to roll over on her back from a dead run, skidding and rolling thru the dirt, coming to a stop in the very middle of big's place...
on her back.

while big was trying to coax sophie to get up and play
little flew thru & snatched the red bone.
when big charged after little, sophie made her escape.
(according to amy, this was a clever plot hatched by sophie & little...in which sophie courageously acted as a decoy)

the dogs have interesting relationships,
sometimes rivals, sometimes playmates, sometimes a team;
and 3 completely different personalities.

the other day we were comparing our dogs to people you might
see at a bar.
sophie would be the one who wouldn't fight, no matter the
provocation.
little would be the runt, who would always be getting into fights
and taking a whipping.
and big would be the guy who would never go into a bar, because
there would always be some drunk idiot who wanted to fight
him.

laz

September 26, 2011
Big's rules for walking (amy)

There are a lot of rules Big has to follow when we go for a run.

> No marking his territory.
> No chasing birds.
> No chasing squirrels.
> No harassing cows or mules.
> No flying after buzzards or dogs.
> No pouncing on toads.

Well, we added 1 more to the list this morning.

Big and I started off in a hurry trying to beat the rain. We've been caught in the rain before and while Big doesn't seem to mind too much, I hate having water drip into my eyes. We had gone just over a mile of our out and back when Big started to drag behind and walk like he needed a restroom break.

While marking his territory isn't allowed on runs, I usually allow him to stop for these special circumstances. I took him over to the side of the road so he could have a little privacy in the ditch. I never even saw it coming. A little field mouse darted right under Big's nose. We'd never singled out chasing field mice as a no-no so Big thought this was fair game. He jumped to the other side of the ditch, tugging his leash out of my hand, but using more than enough force to send me toppling into the ditch. The mouse never stood a chance.

Of course I grabbed Big's leash before he could run off and dragged him back to the road, field mouse dangling limply from his jaws. "Drop!" Big thought this meant "try and swallow it whole!" Field mice are apparently tough to eat in this manner.

Laz thought the whole tale was rather hilarious and thought it worthy of retelling on the list. "Eventually," he said, "Big will think he's not allowed to chase anything."

Amy

september 27, 2011
big's customer service department

i think,
but i can't be sure,
that big would be suprised to find out that team big runners are
carrying his likeness around the country...
and apparently even the world.
but who knows what secrets he keeps,
or how much he knows.

but i do know he would approve
(only regretting that he can't do the "big lean" against every one
of them)
because his big heart seems to have room for all people.
his checkered past has left him cautious.
i am sorry to say, he knows the mean things people are capable
of doing but it has not lessened his affection for them in the least.

it does my heart good to think about team big popping up
everywhere.
they might run the gamut when it comes to speed,
but it is truly an elite team.
should other people want to join,
there are still a few shirts left
(and more can be made if it comes to that)

i have sort of a financial interest,
but all the proceeds will go to big (he has his own bank account)
with hopes of eventually having enough to fence in an area
where he can be free of his cable
(with a fence that will contain him)

sometimes i wonder about the person who abandoned him here
in the woods.
if he had any idea what he was giving up.
i know that the best dogs are often the worst dogs.
with his intelligence, his need for companionship,
and his powerful drive to serve his master;
big would have been a nightmare if he was neglected.

i like to think that he knew big was special, and simply was
unable to meet the demands of owning such a dog.

so he elected to give big a chance, no matter how small.
big is very polite,
and he never stares directly at me.
but sometimes he will be sitting between my feet
(the closest he can get to being a lap dog)
and lean his head back so i can rub his throat
and he will look into my eyes for just a moment or two.

i hope that person who dumped him remembers that look when
he tries to sleep.

laz

september 28, 2011
Big covert ops

i have to admit i was a little worried when little & i got home
from finishing the big trail.
(yes, FINISHING! complete at last, thank god almighty, it's
complete at last)

there was a string of responses in my e-mail about team big,
even one from dave.
i was afraid that my favorite canine rd was getting booted!
instead it was an array of places that team big was making an
appearance.
(just another chapter in the inspiring rags to riches story of an
ugly red dog with a heart of gold)
and the great suggestion that we collect pictures of big's many
friends wearing his colours around the country
(or even the world).
i bet we can get a page for those pictures on his website.
i had already been considering posting all his stories there.

anyway...

i have been worried about how to keep big mentally challenged
(other than figuring out how to escape)
but it seems that little might have that covered.
figuring out how to thwart little's thefts must be occupying a lot
of big's time lately.

when shannon came to help on the trail last weekend,
she brought a sack of bones for big.
i had been giving him one before little and i went out to work on
the trail.
he would take them with great gusto,
and by the time we got back at the end of the day
nothing remained but small fragments scattered about.
little, of course, would snatch them one by one, to big's
consternation.
but big was getting the most use out of them...
or that is how i saw it.

big might have had other ideas.
this morning, when i gave him his bone, he took it.
but instead of digging in, he dropped it on the ground between his feet and sat there looking thoughtful.

when big is thinking it usually means trouble.
so before i changed into my work clothes i peeked out the window to see what he was up to.
he was walking around his area with the bone in his mouth.
while i watched,
he walked over and dropped the bone into his woodpile.
then he stood there looking at it.

(big has a woodpile on one side of his area, from which he sometimes selects a log or board to play with. as carl said one day while watching big drag an 8 foot long board out of the pile, "every dog gets the urge to play with a 2x12 now and then.")

after i changed, i looked again, and big was up to something odd on the other side of his pen.
big was so focused, he didn't even notice me coming out for a better look.

at the back of his pen there is a tree with a couple of buttressed roots forming a 'V' at the base.
he was using his nose to push loose earth into a pile inside the 'V'
then he was tamping it down with his nose.
(he has a nice wide nose for the task)
he would survey his work,
then add more dirt and tamp it down some more.
a quick recon of his area revealed no bone.
not even in the woodpile.

now, i have seen a dog bury a bone before.
they scrape out a shallow hole, drop in the bone,
scratch a little dirt back over it,
and walk away with the bone about half covered.
big was not only burying his bone, he was disguising the cache.

when little & i left, big was still hard at work.
he didn't even bark to tell me i was taking the wrong dog.

at the end of the day, i had to go check out big's handiwork.
i could only shake my head in amazement.
he had finished off by putting loose leaves on top of his tamped
down dirt pile.
i have to admit, if i didn't know it was there, i'd have never seen
anything out of the ordinary.
that dog freaks me out sometimes.

at least he isn't a practiced sneak.
when i got close to his hidey hole, big came scurrying over
and stood there shifting his weight from side to side & looking
worried.

amy came out while big was eating, and i took her over to show
her big's handiwork,
he quit eating immediately, and repeated his nervous hovering.

needless to say, we didn't bother his stash
and gave him an extra dose of loving
(there is a lot of pressure. we are petting for the whole big team)

i'm just not sure how well his plan worked out.
we got a lot of rain tonight.
i don't know if big considered drainage while he was
constructing his hiding place.
it remains to be seen what the condition of his bone will be when
he decides to retrieve it.

of course, that may not matter.
i might have missed the point altogether.
this time the big outwitted the little.

laz

october 03, 2011
big's new toy

big is getting a new toy today.
he removed his dogproof collar one time too many.

we started our game of "come when called/catch me if you can"
at the house.
sandra had just left and called me within less than a minute.
i was expecting some assigned task for the day,
instead i heard, "big is out here in the driveway with me."
"ok, i'll be right there."

i thought about putting on my boots,
but decided that i didn't need to leave an irritated woman and a
free spirited dog alone in the driveway too long
so i went out in my houseshoes.

sandra was stopped in her car just visible in the first curve,
and big was standing outside the car, sniffing in the grass.
things started well enough.
i called big, he came running.
i actually had my hand on him, but he was collarless & i didn't
have a grip yet...
when sandra started down the drive.
tantalizingly close to having had a hold on my dog
i watched him turn and race down the driveway after the
irresistible temptation of the moving car.
"big, big, STOP"
big stopped and looked back, laughter in his eyes.
but, as i approached, he took off again.

big *loves* this game.

i went back to the house and retrieved his collar.
again i passed up putting on my boots as too time consuming.
one of big's humans needs to be in sight if he runs into a
neighbor.
i don't think they will shoot him if i am there.
most of the neighbors have come to like big.

a few remain convinced that he is a latent killer,
just waiting to go berserk.
some have cows, and i understand that if big should decide he
wants to chase cows,
his game will have a very unfunny end.

and so we went. down the drive. all the way to the road.
big would stop and sniff about
but as i approached he would take off again.
"this is not funny, big."

big's grinning face & laughing eyes replied, "yes it is!"
he started to go right when we reached the road,
towards the home of lynnor's pug.
that would not be good.

sometimes when i am returning from my walk, their 2nd grader
will be waiting for the bus.
one day, in the innocent way of 7 year olds, he told me his dad
had said he would "feed that dog some gunpowder."
i don't think he actually realized what that meant.
(any more than his dad realized that tiny ears were listening)

instead, big went down the road towards mr winston's farm,
his favorite playground when he goes renegade.
i was contemplating the ill effects of going into the cow pastures
in my houseshoes
when i saw amy & sophie running up the road towards me.
"ah, someone who can actually run!"

i gave amy the collar & took sophie, then sophie & i settled in to
watch the chase.
from the winston's gate there is a panoramic view of the whole
valley.
amy & big continued the game all the way up the drive,
big stopping to wag his tail at the winston dogs cowering on the
porch,
then the game turned towards the pasture.
i was hoping big would get zapped by the electric fence,
but he passed it unscathed.
it was either off, or he got lucky & went under between pulses.

212

the pair crossed the pasture & first big, then amy, disappeared
into the woods.
there was a long period with no clue about the action,
except amy's occaisional faint calls, "big, come here big. come
here *now*... this is not funny big!"

finally i saw a familiar red shape emerge back into the pasture.
shortly afterwards amy followed.
they made their way back around the woods thru the pasture,
amy getting within arms length several times
before big shot away.

god, he loves this game...
jerk.

when they got back to the electric fence, either the luck of the big
ran out...or mr winston was watching the show from his house
and turned the fence on.

big stopped suddenly, turned and began running towards me at
top speed.
then the sound got to me
a loud "YIPE!"
followed by amy's laughter.

big never slowed down as he made a beeline directly to me,
i reckon he knew exactly where i was all along.

apparently the game was over,
but i got a good grip on the scruff of his neck.
"mr big, i think you done used up your walk today."
a subdued big peacefully waited until amy arrived.
"guess who is getting a harness today, mr big?"

so the big dog is sitting out in his big house right now,
looking mournfully out the door.
his thoughts are easy to read:
"i don't think i am getting a walk today."

but he will have a new challenge to occupy his mind once amy
gets home.

we'll see just how long it takes him to defeat a harness.
seemingly it would be impossible for him to remove,
but thats what they said about the dogproof collar...
and the chain link fence...
and the reinforced crate...

my money is on the big.

laz

october 04, 2011
what was the big betting line?

we didn't have time to put out the over/under on big vs the
harness.

this isn't big's first rodeo,
and he seems to have met the harness before.
i put it on as tight as seemed reasonable,
but after his & amy's run
i observed big squirming about his area...

kind of reminded me of films of harry houdini in a straitjacket.

i almost felt sorry for him.
he has been so creative & ingenious
i sort of hated to see him defeated...

in less than an hour there was an inside out harness
looking rather lonesome lying on the end of a cable.
and a big red evil genius heading down the driveway,
amy in pursuit.

he was betrayed by biology.
amy observed big go into a familiar squatting pose,
kicked in her lifetime best 40 yard dash
and tackled him.
amy is certain she is the first girl ever to tackle a pit bull taking a
dump.

now he's back on his cable
with a skin-tight harness.
we'll give it one more chance.

he shouldn't challenge it for a while.
amy gave him a rhinocerous leg bone.

he is fully occupied trying to find a place to bury it.
the ground is too dam rocky to dig a large enough hole...

215

and even as i write, he came up with a plan.
he moved his woodpile,
scratched out what little hole he could,
put the bone in it
and now is pushing the wood pile back on top with his nose.

he took the sticks in his mouth, one by one
laid them back on top.
and is using his nose to try and get them lined up
this is not really a dog.

it will take a while to get the wood stacked up to his satisfaction.
after that does anyone want to bet on the skin tight harness?

so far the dogproof collar has the highest mark.
it took him a week to figure that one out...
it works like a chinese finger puzzle,
the harder you pull the tighter it gets.

i wonder if big has enough money for an electric fence?

laz

216

october 04. 2011
What was The big betting line (amy)

Laz left out that I started my pursuit in flip-flops and ended it barefoot. Big decided that he doesn't trust the woodpiles hiding spot, possibly because he saw us watching. The bone has been pulled out and he's currently looking for a new spot.

I can see him thinking.

Thank god I'm on his good side.

Amy

october 05, 2011
big and the hand axe

the under 24 hours for total defeat bettors can collect their
winnings.
the harness is disgraced,
(and deceased)
being discovered this morning
sprawled on the ground mortally wounded.

big was waiting at the door.

upon examination, it appears the neckpiece was severed cleanly
with a sharp object.
or maybe he managed to snap it.

usually big performs his amazing feats while no one is looking,
but after we ratcheted the harness to skin tight
he revealed his technique for removing it
(ok, we surreptitiously spied on him thru the window)

the harness is simple, really.
2 belts; one around the neck and one around the chest
connected by a breastplate and a strap down the back.
big simply went to the end of his cable,
turned sideways
and then pulled until the harness was sideways.
the breastplate only pulled up into his armpit,
but the backstrap was down far enough for him to pull his arm
up under it.
from there various contortions (the wriggling i witnessed)
would get his elbow under the back (now side) strap.
after that he could get that leg behind the strap
and pull the harness off inside out.

after we embedded the chest strap into his flesh,
that technique did not work.

so i went to bed thinking my worst problem was how to keep the
chest strap from becoming permanently embedded.

219

wrong.

first we thought he had chewed his way out.
but seeing it was the neckpiece that was severed, that was
impossible.

besides, upon closer examination,
the loose ends were cleanly parted.

definitely not chewed.

he had to have simply snapped it...

except the strap looked much more like it had been cut with a
sharp object.

then we discovered what looks like a crude stone tool...

laz

october 08, 2011
big pee-mails and little bowling

i guess i should start with the big trail update.
little & i completed the course marking today.
it might be the best marked trail in ultrarunning.
there will never be a time that the next course marking is not
visible.

even geraldi & price couldn't get lost...
unless they team up.

yesterday big took his turn doing the course for time.
he notched a 1:48:29.
he missed little's time by 5:08,
but big faced several handicaps.
big had to do the trail on a leash.

little will trot just ahead of me, stopping at intersections
and waiting to see which way we are going.
big is a mite too independent for that,
he'll just pick his own route, and i can follow if i wish.

big did rattlesnake duty for about 3 miles,
but leading on a leash on trail is very demanding.
he has to go fast enough that i don't run into him,
but slow enough not to pull.

it is a pretty tough trick for a big,
the last mile or so big was pretty well pooped,
so he chose to follow,
it was about 85 degrees,
and he just doesn't tolerate heat over the long haul.
also he ended up doing 5, instead of 4.1666667 miles.

the first time we started, ben's wife came by while we were
finishing up the road portion. our social obligation to stop & talk
ruined his time, so we started over.
but none of that was why he couldnt beat little's time.

big (being a modern dog) is all over the social media, and kept stopping to send his pee mails.
they all have the same message, of course, "this is big's trail!"

even on the return trip over the same trail we had to make our stops, so he could re-read his own pee mails

one or two must have had typo's,
because he needed to edit them.

leaving big to lay in the shade & be wasted,
i took little for another 5 miles.
the heat was an even bigger issue at that point.
little would pull ahead to get to each shady stretch,
and then drag behind when we were about to enter the sun.
we passed the short creek church with about a mile & a half to go
and i soaked little with their hose.

she was not all that appreciative, but it did cool her down.
i left little in the pen to lay in the shade & be wasted
and went inside to revel over my 10 mile day...
and get ready for basketball practice.

after practice, it was time to bring little & sophie in for supper.
the dogs were recovered by then.
big was gnawing on his mastodon leg bone,
and little was waiting for the chance to steal it.

amy got sophie out first.
sophie has to come out of the pen on a leash,
or she will run straight to the cow pasture for a cow-pie beauty
treatment. (god only knows why amy insists on washing it off)
if she doesn't get to roll in cow poop the next best thing is to
wrap her leash around your legs & try to pull you down.

i got a hearty laugh out of watching amy stumbling across the
yard with sophie...
not suspecting that i was about to repay the favor.
little is always wound too tight.
any additional excitement,

such as someone arriving at the house, supper time, getting out
of the pen... or stealing big's bone... totally overwhelms her.
she tucks her butt and runs in circles at about 50 miles an hour
to release the excess energy.

i was prepared for her to shoot out of the pen when i gave her
release command, and head straight for big's area.
true to form, that was exactly what she did.
big leapt to his feet and jumped between his bone and the on-
rushing little
(in what would have been a futile attempt to defend it)

i was ready, and stopped little with a command
(feeling slightly smug that *my* dog was under voice control)
being denied the chance to snatch big's bone only wound little
tighter.
she came back & started tearing thru the woods in huge circles
(i have no idea how she avoids hitting a tree)
having long since figured out that it is in my best interest to let
little burn off as much energy as possible
i just watched.

after a couple of hell for leather loops thru the woods
little hit the driveway & was roaring back
(still going about 50 miles an hour)
as she crossed the backyard i realized that she was headed for
big's area again.
(i only told her not to go straight back there and steal big's bone.
i didn't tell her she couldnt run in circles and then steal big's
bone... right?)
thinking to myself, "you little jerk"
i stepped into little's path.
i didn't have time to come up with a really good plan.
i didn't give a lot of thought to what would happen when a 40
pound furry bowling ball, traveling at 50 miles an hour, hit my
ankles.

now i can tell you how a bowling pin feels.
my feet were instantly knocked out from under me
rotating me around, with my belt buckle as the pivot point,
leaving my body parallel with the ground.

this is not a sustainable position.
the last part of the physics demonstration was gravity
and i came to earth rather quickly.

amy said i fell with the grace of a big cat... ok, maybe those
weren't her exact words but i am sure that is what she meant.

[*That's exactly what "like watching a sack of feed corn hit the
ground" means. -Amy*]

fortunately, i was scarcely aware of most of the impact,
focusing all my attention on my right knee
due to the kneecap's collision with a rock.

i rolled around on the ground, clutching my knee and practicing
all the swear words i know. behind me i could hear amy making
choking noises (maybe she was having some sort of seizure? no
way she was laughing at me!)

by the time i had run through my entire supply of swear words
amy had regained her composure enough to ask, "are you all
right?"
"sure. i'm great. i just fractured my ******* kneecap!"

then i remembered little & big's bone.
big was still standing in front of his bone;
looking at us like we were all crazy.
little was laying on the ground about 10 feet past where i had
been standing,
looking dazed

if she had a brain, she'd have probably gotten a concussion.
amy tried to make me feel better, "if only i had a video of that."

i think the listers are right.
we need to set up a camera & produce dog-training videos.
i'm not sure anyone else does it quite the way we do.
the way most people do it,
the dog is the one doing amazing tricks.

laz (don't try this trick at home. we are trained professionals)

224

october 19, 2011
big's tentative truce

all he wanted was his blanket back.

as big's friends are well aware,
containing big is no small feat.
he wont tolerate being enclosed,
and has demonstrated the ability to defeat any latch,
any door, any wall or fence meant to deprive him of his freedom.
and he doesn't rest until he is out.

we finally compromised with his cable.
he will tolerate being restricted, as long as he isn't enclosed...

to a point.

if big feels like he isn't being treated right,
he will escape the cable & come looking for us.
with his thick neck,
the only way we could keep a regular collar on at all
was to tighten it so tight that he could barely breath.

we found the "dogproof" collar,
which he will generally tolerate.
but he can remove it when he really wants to.

the last time it rained for more than two days,
big decided he had enough,
and removed his "dogproof" collar repeatedly.

so we decided to go to a harness,
figuring we had to be the ones who decided whether big was on
his cable, or at the back door looking in.

the harness was a debacle.
before we ever met him, big had obviously mastered the harness.

so we put him back on the "dogproof" collar,
and a tentative truce was called.

225

we made sure big got his walks & attention,
and he acted like he was contained.

last week it rained a couple of times.
big has a blanket that he keeps in his house to lay on,
however, when the ground is wet
he will bring it out and spread it on the ground to lay on.
that is all well and good,
except he seldom remembers to put it back up when it rains
again.
usually i put it back for him,
but last week, when it rained twice on the same day,
his blanket was out & got soaked.

so i hung it up on the porch to dry.
(don't tell big, but it stinks too bad to go in the dryer.
i value my life more than to do that)

last night it rained, and finally turned cold.
this morning was downright chilly.

everything started out like normal.
amy & sophie ran (while big voiced his displeasure)
then big & i walked...
not a long day today, altho he made it clear he wanted to go on
one of our longer routes.
then he got fed...
after which he generally retires to his house for a morning nap.

not today.

he complained and complained while little & i started our walk.
when little & i reached halfway down the hill, big finally stopped
barking.
"good," i told little, "i guess big has settled down."
i couldnt have been more wrong.
big was taking his collar off, so he could come & get me.
as little & i approached the road, i heard a sound like a freight
train coming down the drive.
it was big.
i was dreading another game of "catch me if you can"

226

but that wasn't big's purpose.
little & i were about to turn around anyway,
since the rain had started back up,
and big came with us
circling us at about 50 miles an hour
(and knocking little down on every lap,
a fun game they like to play)

once i got little in the house,
i sat on the back step & big sat between my feet and laid his head
in my lap.
i figured he just needed some extra attention,
so i sat there with him quite a while.
finally, it came time i needed to move on
so i told him, "ok mr big, its time to go back to your house."

big didn't complain.
he got up and walked over to his partially dried blanket and
sniffed at it.
then he looked at me,
then back at the blanket,
message sent, he came back over to me.

"it's still kind of wet, big. but i guess it's better than nothing."
i took him back, put him on his cable, and put his damp blanket
back in his house.
satisfied, big went in & curled up for his morning nap.
he just wanted his blanket back.

so we don't really keep big on a cable.
we have a tentative truce
where he pretends that the cable holds him,
as long as we keep things in their proper order.

big knows how to manage people.
i can almost hear him telling little;
"the important thing is that they always think they are in charge."

laz

october 23, 2011
hour 0, the big death match approaches

big was incredulous when i brought his food out before we
walked.
eating is scheduled for after walking.
he ate a few bites, just to be polite.
but it was time for a walk.

when we got to the bottom of the hill, the schedule was shot.
strange structures had been added to the familiar lawn,
and new people were adding more.
instead of the expected walk, there was a little socializing,
and then big was attached to his cable...
which had been moved to the telephone pole down by the little
house.

even if the routine had been altered
all in all, it was a good day for big.
part of the time sleeping in the sun,
interspersed with greeting a mix of strangers & old friends
and watching the odd goings on.
best of all, the master was always around
stopping by frequently to make that all important contact.

his walk finally came in the afternoon.
it wasn't quite like any walk he'd taken before,
there was a large crowd accompanying us.

one of them apparently didn't understand the proper order of
things
(and how important it is for things to be in the proper order)
he kept walking in front of big
(something only the master is supposed to do)
even tho big was very polite and never looked directly at the
subversive, he was forced to pull on the leash to try and correct
things.

once we hit big's beloved trail, matters improved.
big was in the lead.

229

he didn't get to split lead time like he usually does,
because the subversive was next in line most of the way.
as far as big was concerned,
it was all around safer to keep the master between big and such a
menacing individual.

after it got dark,
amy took big back up to his bigloo
where he could rest easy in the comfort of familiarity,
and listen to the people sounds drifting up from the bottom of
the hill.

for the rest of us the day was built around setting up for the race
and watching the gypsy camp sprout on the lawn.
after dark we had a nice campfire going,
and sat up late speculating on what the morrow would bring.

one by one, people drited off to their tents,
until the last few finally departed,
leaving only smoldering embers under the stars.

when the sun returned, the death match would begin.

laz

october 24, 2011
hour 1, big and the infinite loop

when amy brought big down, just before sunup,
the lawn of the little house was transformed.
a mob of runners was milling about,
tents, tables, chairs, and coolers were scattered all about,
and colorful flags lined the driveway.

big had never seen anything quite like this.
a few people stopped to pet him,
but he was watching the whole thing with a certain unease.

minutes before the sun peeked over the horizon,
a series of whistle blasts signaled most of the crowd to gather in
the drive.

precisely at the moment the first rays of sunlight arrived,
a loud bell sent the whole mass charging off down the road.
big was relieved when we started back up the hill.
it would be nice to retreat to the safety of his bigloo and
contemplate all the strangeness.
he did tentatively test, to see if we might be going on the trail
again, but instead we walked a few steps past the trail, and then
stopped, looking back down the driveway.

after a couple of minutes,
big's worst fears were realized.
all those people were coming back,
and this time they were running directly at *him!*

the first few turned at the last minute,
but more were behind them
and when we continued towards the house he was pulling like a
crazed tractor.

when we reached my car, he begged to get in.
then he tried to go up on the porch
and then to go inside his bigloo.
unfortunately master was not really grasping the level of fear

and took the poor big on to where the trail passed behind the house. a few minutes later, all those runners went charging past again.

to make matters worse, after that ordeal was finished, we walked on to the bottom of the hill, big pulling frantically, trying to get as far from the runners as possible,
when what should happen,
but they all came back yet again, this time from in front of him.
master did catch on that big was about out of control,
and waited for the last runner to pass before starting back.

big really wanted to retreat to his beloved bigloo.
instead he found it moved down to the bottom of the hill...
along with his water bowl and his new bone.
the whole world was turned upside down.

josh, who has been a great source of information about dogs,
later explained to me that when a dog has been frightened it can take a couple of hours or more for the adrenaline to subside.
the unfortunate big never got that sort of temporal luxury
as a new flood of runners erupted past him every hour,
replenishing his supply of adrenaline and he spent a miserable, terrified day standing in front of his bigloo
warning everyone,
even old friends,
to keep their distance.
big's confidence in his master is not always well-founded.
with a little better planning this could have been a glorious day for big, who loves nothing more than meeting new people (especially the ladies).
instead, he was trapped in an infinite loop.

but big wasn't alone in the infinite loop.
more than a third of the backyarders finished the out section successfully,
finished the loop successfully,
and then, instead of heading onto the back section,
began another loop,
running anything from a few yards to an entire loop before realizing their error.

sal coll led the way among the directionally competent, finishing the 4.166667 miles in 42:22
(winning the meaningless first race by more than 3 minutes)

21 of the 32 runners who started the loop finished it within the time limit. (abi meadows dropped after walking the half mile from the parking lot)

11 directionally challenged runners went slightly over the time limit, including several contenders.
in a quick race-day adjustment, those runners were allowed to continue and make up the time on loop 2.

juli decided against going for it, and settled in for the day.
only an hour in the bank and 33 runners had already been reduced to 31.

at the time, it seemed that the format would not begin to be difficult for many hours.
that prediction could not have been more wrong.

laz

october 25, 2011
small actions speak louder than big words

big's race was over, and the last runners were packing to go.
we were down starting the task of cleaning up the aftermath.

the race had been a success,
but it had not been a great day for big.
too many people,
too much disruption of his normal schedule,
and too much excitement.
big had not had much fun.

the day before the race he had been his charming self.
and now on the day after, he was finally relaxed again.

as we stood in a circle, talking,
big was making his rounds.
he would walk up to each person and make himself available for
petting.

as if attracted by magnetic force,
hardly realizing they were doing it
each person would pet him for a few minutes,
then big would move on.
as he had since he first came to the house in the woods,
big included Sandra on every round.

Sandra was always the pragmatic one.
she insisted that we could not keep this big ugly dog.
she never stopped asking when i would find him a permanent
home.

she had warned me not to "become too attached."
she had followed her own advice,
always keeping her distance from the big dog.

but big was a champion charmer.
he was never pushy,
he simply never gave up making himself available for affection.

and he had done something even more important.
his protective attitude towards sandra's child
had won him big points.

as i watched,
Sandra leaned over and patted that monstrous head.
big fairly beamed with pleasure.

when my turn came, i leaned over and whispered in his ear.
"you have won, mr big. you are home to stay."
as he leaned against me i couldnt help believing that big knew.
his quest was over.

laz

postscript:

january 10, 2011
the big tail tale

i remember commenting when big had first come to stay at the
house on the hill
that big did not wag his tail very much.
after little, who wags her tail all day long (and wags the whole
back half of her body when she is especially happy)
big just struck me as a much more reserved dog.

this morning, after our rain shortened walk,
big and i were spending some time on the porch.
big had finished eating, and already done some time sitting
between my feet getting petted,
so he was just walking around the porch checking things out.

each time he came to one of his own things, he wagged his tail.
he sniffed at his spare dry blanket, and wagged his tail.
he sniffed at his prized blue leash, and wagged his tail.
i told him, "you've become quite the tail-wagger, havent you?"
big looked at me...

and wagged his tail.

big is a changed dog from the one that showed up here a year
and a half ago.
when big got here, his coat was dull and dry and he was riddled
with parasites.
big today has a shiny coat, and is in robust health
(save for the catch in his shoulder)
but the real difference is a little harder to put a finger on.

big has never wavered in his optimistic outlook.
he has never stopped being charming and affectionate.
his enthusiasm and that twisted sense of humor have always
been part of the big package.
but something about him had changed,
and i just couldnt put my finger on it.

he loves his possesions...
his bigloo, his aboveground pool, his chaise lounge, his precious
blue leash, his blankets, and even the cable & dogproof collar that
he can remove at will.

but those were not the reason he rescued me from not owning a
big.

big craved a place he belonged, and a master he belonged to.

the difference in big today is subtle.
it would be hard to pinpoint a change in the things he does...

it is his tail that tells the tale.

big no longer has faith that he will find his place in the world.
he believes he already has.

laz

About the Author

Lazarus Lake did not write this book; he merely recorded the stories that Big shared with him. They live on a farm in Tennessee where they train and organize popular ultramarathons, a world-wide community that Laz has been a part of for over 3 decades and Big first joined a couple of years ago.

About the Illustrator

Betsy Julian lives with her musician husband, striped cat, and opinionated cockatiel in the hills of East Tennessee. She has a BFA and a MS in Education. Her art is inspired by traditional Appalachian applied arts. Most of the time she can be found in a ceramics studio or teaching high school art.

About the Designer

Blaine Moore is a competetive runner and marathon coach in Southern Maine and writes online at the popular website, RunToWin.com. His publishing company helps authors get their books in print. Learn more at: TrailTrotterPress.com

Made in the USA
Lexington, KY
01 March 2012